HUSHED SKIES & FLOATING NIGHTS

FABLES, POETRY, AND MAGIC

MEGHA KAUSHIK

This book has been published with all efforts taken to make the material error-free after the consent of the author. However, the author and the publisher do not assume and hereby disclaim any liability to any party for any loss, damage, or disruption caused by errors or omissions, whether such errors or omissions result from negligence, accident, or any other cause.

While every effort has been made to avoid any mistake or omission, this publication is being sold on the condition and understanding that neither the author nor the publishers or printers would be liable in any manner to any person by reason of any mistake or omission in this publication or for any action taken or omitted to be taken or advice rendered or accepted on the basis of this work. For any defect in printing or binding the publishers will be liable only to replace the defective copy by another copy of this work then available.

for the soul that has always loved me,

held me, and stood by me.

Contents

Preface

my heart ripped me out of my lonliness and hushed thoughts
my mind went numb as i pondered over the hundered fables
just to find the most beautiful ones, the ones which
melts into the floating nights like nothing but poetry
this book presents to you the awakening, the illumination
the magic and the enchantment, the memories and fables,
the dreams and lonliness of the hushed skies
and the floating nights

1. the lonliness

to live for,
the hope of it all

forever trying
to reconcile this hopelessly
romantic heart, and this fiercely
independent soul
i'm such a soft lover,
and a wild wanderer
but i think you're where
all of me finds home

it's always the ones you love
that teach you never to

i'll always be someplace
i never want to be

you left and this once

all the pieces of my heart
fell back together
instead of falling into bits

i'm not dead yet
but i shall soon be immortalized
as the perpetual nightmare
that snaps the door to your only escape
shut right in front of your face
don't get me wrong though,
for vendetta is the last thing
on my mind right now;
tonight, i'm not concocting a potion of revenge
for this night is all about freedom
not from you, but from myself
because you could never satiate the hunger
my belly holds for absolution
and i don't even need to enclose myself
with candles or cast a spell
all i need is the fury that flows in my veins
anger is always more than enough
to incite a hex of rebellion anyway,
and the chalice is already filled
to the brim with my blood,
the pale moonlight is falling in soft waves
over the vessel of precious metal,

the moon being the sole witness to
the revolution brewing tonight
and my body has never felt more alive
now i'm here, minutes away from raising
the naïve little girl you killed,
back from the dead but don't worry,
because she's not here to get her revenge,
she's merely here to make history

every beautiful
poetry is the battle cry
of many unsung heroes

every spoken word
is a message from a dead poet

every iambic meter
is a language of
a dead poet's soul

every powerful word
a poet scribbles is an
expression of the soul and
a reflection of what it has to say

anxiety doesn't attack
it kills me
and brings me back to life
i understand why - i am so resilient
i die a thousand times
and still, live

is it just a teardrop falling
from my eyelashes on my palm
or the screams of my tired soul
that i have confined for so long?
forgive me for letting my emotions
flow from the valleys of heartbreaks,
but the ocean inside
now feels overburdened,
this flood within is now too heavy
for me to carry

i would smile for you
as and when you say,
suppressing all my sorrows
under the little happiness, i've got
but, some days the volcano in me
bursts the fire out,
for the suffocation inside choke my lungs
and now they long to inhale freely

my mother injects power into me
wiping off my tears,
claiming i am bold enough
to net let these adversities drown me
but, even the happiest flowers
are destined to wilt someday,
even the toughest person
melts sometime

what else should i do
other than letting it all out,
when my arteries turn cold
the blood doesn't want to flow,
it aches like the stones being pelted
over my head continuously,
the knife piercing my heart,
can i cry for a while?
the clouds too let it flow,
for they know
sometimes all we can do is
mourn over a few things
only if crying was a curse,
the rain would never be loved

lately, the stars of my fate
have found some loneliness
in the universe
whom they've hugged
with the warmth of my griefs,
for it's always the one
whose heart has been torn apart,
who understands the pain
of being shattered
and having no one to mourn with

i have been chasing
the wrong clouds all my life
while i deserve to create a sky of my own
this agony called life
now consumes me
in tiny crunches every day,
yet some part of me
wishes to soar high
like those birds and
shine like the morning light
sometimes these tiny seeds of hope
are enough to let the flowers
of perseverance
the rise in the barred lands
of my despair

since forever,
i share my wretchedness with the moon
and she always reminds me,
how everyone is born with the void
having no one around,
yet the power to shine
resides in one's soul

the moon too is lost among the stars,
yet she is loved
for always flaunting her scars
you see, no pain is ever too much
to dim your capacity to shine
loneliness sometimes,
is an opportunity to stand out
and rule the world
with your unique struggles

some days i am a mountain,
some days i am just a ocean of tears

though in pieces;
darling, you're every bit a beautiful art

i thought i found
the missing piece, when i met you
but turned out
it was the wrong puzzle

take your time,
don't worry
i'll wait forever
if that is what
it'll take you,
to love me

if it wasn't in the destiny of blues
to be born as a metaphor for sorrows,
perhaps, it would be for the
yellow petals of dandelions in summer
the thing is,
it wouldn't cease to exist

there are so many things
that fascinates me
about the existence of different faces
with different thoughts
having similar body compositions
yet discriminative behavior

the dark shades of any human
are inevitable,
and so are the brighter ones

everyone takes birth
with a single identical heart,
that grows up beating for different people
if that doesn't sound
beautiful happening to mankind,
then perhaps, we need to learn
to admire the serenities of life

i read somewhere,
people will love you till you're good,
that stuck in my head for so long
till i fell in love
with someone i never liked
the facet of human love is,
when we love someone
with our whole hearts,
their little actions form a home
somewhere in your soul,
regardless of the immorality they've

the more people you meet,
the more you realize
that none out there shines brightly

without having themselves burnt
people aren't good and bad,
their deeds are
even the worst times come with
little serendipities,
even the worst phases
of the people
come with hidden
worthiness in them

but when i'm empty,
God,
will you still
pour out of me,
more than me?

around this time you realize
that you are not okay
that everyone around you
is safe in their dreams
while you are kept awake by all the demons
that don't let you sleep
your thoughts begin to spiral
and downward you go,
as soon as your first tear falls,

it's like you've called in a storm
your heart is in tangles
and your mind is a mess,
you find yourself scattered, drowning in a sea
of your own sadness
and now you lay awake wishing
you spent the night counting stars,
instead of all the problems in your life

it's midnight and i'm lying here
crying about nothing,
but at the same time, it's everything
nothing's wrong,
but nothing's right, either

some days,
i feel everything at once
other days,
i feel nothing at all
i don't know what's worse:
drowning beneath the waves
or dying from thirst

you are the kindest thing that

ever happened to me,
even if that is not how our tale is told
when everyone else told me
i was destined to be a
forgotten nymph
that nurtured flowers and
turn meadows gold,
you saw that the ichor that resides in me
demanded its own throne
you showed me
how a love like ours
can turn even the darkest,
the coldest realm into
the happiest of homes

if the sky knew half
of what we're doing down here
it would be stricken,
inconsolable,
and we would have
nothing but rain

it wasn't with knives
my heart tore,
when he brought me to death's door

it wasn't his hands
that had me slain
but he had killed me all the same
Cold and callous
with no remorse,
he turned me into a walking corpse
and i am imprisoned
in this pain,
while he without
the slightest blame
free to do it
over again

there are silences inside you
that you have yet to explore
there are things inside you
that are still fighting a war
some days will be unkind
some days you will want to forget
but stay for those days
that is worth more than all the rest
be easy on your soul
it needs softness
it needs time
it needs patience

there is a quiet in my heart,
like one who rests from days of pain outside,
the sparrows on the roof are chirping
in the dripping rain rain in my heart;
rain on the roof;
and memory sleeps beneath the gray
and windless sky and brings no dreams
of any well remembered day i would not have
the heavens fair, nor golden clouds,
nor breezes mild, but days like this,
until my heart to loss of you is reconciled
i would not see you every hope to know you
as you were has ranged i, who am altered,
would not find the face
i loved so greatly changed

in a crowded room never felt lonelier
no one understands only her
wishing they would listen
skin beginning to glisten from the bloody wounds
of her own self-deprecation
manifesting self-made internal damnation
with no escape again i'm trapped

we choose
to stay numb
because we think it keeps us safe
but the most dangerous thing we can do
is forget how to feel

i love you in the autumn
between the ghostly birch trees
and underneath the changing leaves
i love you in the shifting winds
and every flock of geese
in cold grey lakes and quiet rains,
i love you in the rustling of the long grass
and the melting of
my frost-bitten heart

we
all
bleed
the
same

in the midst of my sadness
i turn to the moon

there is a kind of lonely
only the night can understand

she walked
through life
with the eyes of a wolf
who belonged to no one
but the night

it was the longest night in winter,
when i sent a question into space,
asking how i'd ever change,
when i'm trapped in the same place,
and i heard the full moon giggle,
as she cloaked me in her light,
along with the same swath of stars,
i looked at every night, i blushed pink as a sunrise,
at the joke i didn't get, until the moon gave me her answer,
in the minutes before she set,
"you have much to learn on standing still,"
she told me with a smile,
"for since you first asked me that question,
you've moved five hundred thousand miles"

she is a lovely dreamer
with eyes of far away foreign lands

tell the demons
i'm home

i hate to be alone
there are too many voices talking

somewhere in the great landscape
of the time
there is a garden growing
the most beautiful rose
that has ever been
and that will ever be
you are that rose, forever to me

for my part
i know nothing
with any certainty
but the sight of the stars
make me dream

and suddenly —
the dreams started chasing me

being is strange
but wonderful too

in the same way that light filters
through the forest trees
she knows even here by her father,
she is seen and even though she has
a long way to go, she knows hell light the path
to lead her safely home

do you remember the night the moon
dropped from the sky? and we ran through
the forest to find where it lie,
i was tripping on tree roots and slipping
on snow, you were holding my hand
saying not to let go, when we found it,
at last, there were twigs in our hair,
a rose on our cheeks and our breath in the air,
and the words to describe it got caught in our throats,
as its silver light danced through

the threads of our coats,
we knew that our eyes had not seen such a view,
you were looking at it,
i was looking at you

i'd write love letters to the earth,
whisper them to the wind,
fold them into paper boats,
and find a stream to sail them in,
i'd write of beautiful sunrises,
of the oranges and pinks,
while i sit beside the seashore,
where the waves can smudge my ink,
i'd write these words on paper,
but for the paper i need trees,
like many things mankind has made,
but doesn't really need,
and so our letters to the earth,
leave less love than they do scars,
when we write them in our blinding light,
that blocks out all the stars,
so when writing letters to the earth,
it's time that we rethink,
since we don't need a piece of paper,
if the life we live's the ink

she wove golden rays of sunshine,
into a long and flowing dress,
that left the scent on everything she touched,
of nature's sweet caress,
everywhere the girl did go,
the flowers would all bloom,
and she could chase the lonely feeling,
out of every darkened room,
she could drive out all your sadness,
and cause a frozen heart to thaw,
she'd paint the sky pink every morning,
but nobody ever saw,
no one thought to thank her,
for the warmth upon their skin,
or for chasing all their demons,
from where the night-time's breath had been,
so she thought she wasn't needed,
she could leave and they'd not care,
but they'd just taken her for granted,
since her light was always there,
because you never thank the ground,
until you know how it feels to fall,
or just how much you need the sun,
until it doesn't rise at all

Poetry is the bridge of words,
over my fire,
i rely upon it

life changes

2. the dreams

we are like the spider.
we weave our life
and then move along in it.
we are like the dreamer
who dreams and then lives
in the dream. this is true,
for the entire universe
- the Upanishads

once upon a time,
there was a little girl who loved to dream.
she would wish upon stars and dream of the future.
she would imagine great happiness
and seek after new hope.
in fact, the little girl spent most of her days
wishing and dreaming and hoping
for things that would make her life a little less ordinary.
the more she dreamed,
the better she felt. and the better she felt
the more she dreamed.
days, weeks, and months passed.
the little girl continued to wish on

the stars and wait for the moment
when one day, her dreams would come true.
however, the little girl was so preoccupied
with her dreaming, that opportunities passed her by
like clouds on the horizon.
one evening when the sky was twinkling
with little stars, she noticed something
floating by her.
it was a little boy clutching desperately
to a rope, which was attached to a sparkling star.
the little girl stared in amazement
before calling out desperately to the boy.
"are you alright?"
the little boy smiled back whilst clutching
onto the rope for dear life.
"what are you doing?" the little girl
exclaimed in wonderment.
"i am catching my wishing star", he replied.
"i am going to make my wishes come true."
the boy surely and steadily began climbing up
the rope towards his star,
as he continued to pass by the little girl.
the little girl looked up in the sky at all the stars
she had ever wished on.
there were millions and millions of them,
each one twinkling so brightly.
not one of those stars had ever fallen into her lap.

not one of her wishes had ever come true.
this time she looked to a new star and made a new wish.
she picked up a rope and with all her might threw
it up into the sky. it wrapped itself around her
chosen star and she grabbed onto it for dear life.
the little girl's life was about to change,
and change for the better,
as she had finally found her ideal.

you are my love story,
and i write you into everything i do,
everything i see,
everything i touch and
everything i dream,
you are the words that fill my pages

if i were the moon,
i would want you to be my night

she had magic in her eyes
even the stars envied

if you came to me with a face

i have not seen, with a voice, i have never heard,
i would still know you.
even if centuries separated us,
i would still feel you.
somewhere between the sand and
the stardust,
through every collapse and creation,
there is a pulse that
echoes of you and me.
when we leave this world,
we give up all our possessions
and our memories.
love is the only thing
we take with us.
it is all we carry from
one life to the next

i feel my life culminating to a point,
the delicate threads of my existence
joining to form a tapestry.
the events up until the present
that had seemed of
no particular significance,
now imbued with a deeper,
darker meaning.
i can see it so clearly-the greater plan.

i understand that i am both the architect
and tenant of my imminent
destruction and rebirth.
i can feel it so acutely like
an ache in my chest,
ultimately knowing i am locked
into a chain of events
that i cannot stop,
an outcome i cannot alter,
feeling at once helpless
yet hopelessly awed
by the power of my part in this beautiful,
brutal expression of the universe.

i have moved so far away from you
that i have become a myth;
a lie you tell yourself each night.
i am the one true thing you've held
in the palm of your hand,
the key to everything you wanted.
your name smiles at me
from a crumpled envelope,
addressed to the past,
unsent and unseen.
inside there is a letter
where i tell you a story

about the moon,
how night after night
the darkness carved at
the pale curve of her body
until she became half the woman she was.
there is a word that hurts my heart-
one i don't ever say out loud.
like the shadow that lingers in the light,
i can't separate myself from your memory.
but there are some nights when i look up into the sky,
and the moon is whole again

"some people don't know what they have until it's gone."
"but what about the ones who do know?
the ones who never took a damn thing for granted?
who tried their hardest to hold on,
yet could only look on helplessly while they lost
the thing they loved the most.
isn't it so much worse for them?"

the days catapult before me.
the world is spinning too quickly.
it gets harder and harder to retrace my steps.
to figure out how i got to be here.
the years expand into eons.

it gets easier for me to imagine
my mother as a girl.
to think about her worn-out
heart-breaking for the things
she couldn't hold on to.
and i wonder if i've let the wrong people go.
when you lose a person,
a whole universe goes along with them.
sometimes i picture all my other selves,
standing in line like
a row of dominoes;
separate but part of the same disjointed whole.
how can i hold a single one accountable?
no one ever walks away from love,
knowing they can never go back.

one day he will find you.
he will touch you and you will feel
a lifetime of the indifference of apathy
melt away in a single moment.
and you will ache for him.
you will love him,
in the way, you walk a tightrope-
in the way people learn
to fall asleep in a war zone.
you will bleed for him until the day he is gone.

you will bleed for him every day after that.
the time will pass and you will feel robbed
you will grow bitter.
you will ask why,
but you won't get an answer.
and that is when the words will come.

you begin to invent things after a while.
i suppose it's only human nature
to add and subtract from our memories;
to recall them the way we feel
they should be remembered.
after all, our lives are a living work of art
shouldn't we be allowed to shape them
in any way we choose?
i remember the first time
i saw my favorite painting,
how its fragile beauty snatched my breath.
and i thought if picasso had painted
just one brushstroke less,
he could have told an entirely different story.
if he began with a smear of red instead of blue,
it could have been a chapter instead of an era.

i have walked through the ruins

of an empire as it fell through
the passageway of time.
i have witnessed star after star
exploding like fireworks,
as i fixed my gaze light years
into the sky.
and i was only a pinprick of dust
on the day they split the atom.
i had yet to learn the most destructive thing
in the world is the quiet yearning
between two people who
long to find their way
back to each other.

i talk to you all the time,
even if you can't hear me.
i tell you constantly,
over and over,
how much i miss you
and that for me,
nothing has changed.
i think about the days when
we could say anything to each other.
my heart is like a time capsule-it keeps me safe,
the memory of you.
i know it's harder with you gone

than if you had never been here at all-
but i wouldn't have missed it for the world.

"don't you get it?" he said.
"the ones who are afraid
of heights don't trust
themselves enough not to jump."

maybe it's okay
to take time to be okay.
maybe it's okay to miss them
on days like this and cry
when it does not make sense
why things had to end that way.
maybe there is room to take
this day by day.
and maybe in that room.
there is endless boundless grace.

he first fear
being drowning, the
ship's first shape was a raft, which
after that didn't
happen. It's awkward to have to do one's

was hard to unflatten planning
in extremis sleekening the hull,
in the early years so hard to hide later:
making things more gracious.

You are telling a story,
How Fire Took Water to Wife
It's always like this, you say,
opposites attract
be one,
so he burns her as hard as he can
They want to enter each other,
and she tries to drown him
It's called love at first and doesn't hurt
But after a while she weeps and says he is killing her.
he shouts that he cannot breathe
underwater
Make up your own ending, you say to the children,
and they will, they will

If only he could touch her,
Her name like an old wish
In the stopped weather of salt On a snail.
He longs to be
Words, juicy as passionfruit On her tongue.

He'd do anything.
Would dance three days & nights
To make the most terrible gods
Rise out of ashes of the yew,
To step from the naked Fray,
to be as tender As meat imagined off
The bluegill's pearlish Bones.
He longs to be An orange,
to feel fingernails Run
a scam through him.

Imagine one night alone,
no longer call my own.
in a bed I that would
All I would be able to feel is your body
intertwined with mine,
with nothing but these satin sheets
to harbor our soft-pressed skin.
You'll rest your head on my favorite pillow,
my face will be buried in your flower-scented neck.
With every touch, I'll move in closer.
With every kiss, our hearts will beat faster.
My fingers will travel through the depths of your hair,
as you allow my lips to graze every inch of your skin.
It will be perfection nonetheless.
And if perfection were to exist,

this would all be incredibly true.
But as I lie on this empty bed
and tend to this starving heart,
i can only wish,
to be here with you.

I imagine our feet brushing
against each other under the sheets
in the early morning.
I imagine sighing your name
against your shoulder.
I imagine slipping my fingers
under your shirt to remind me
of how lucky I got to be the one
touching your skin.

I love how you hold me.
I love how you tell me I‘m beautiful.
I love how you find it funny when I say something stupid
or just can't speak when I'm around you.
I love how you make me happy.
I love how you smile when I see you.
I love how you laugh when I say something random, or stupid.
I love that when I laugh it makes you smile.

I love how you ask me if I'm alright
when I can't stop laughing.
I love how you make me feel.
I love how you tell me I look cute.
I love how we can talk about randomness for hours.
I love that you want to stay up late into the night.
I love how you say sweet things to me.
I love how you whisper in my ear when we hug.
I love how you squeeze me so hard when I hug you.
I love how I can talk to you for hours about anything,
and you listen, and I listen.
I love how you want to spend every day with me.
I love how you caress my hand.
I love how you hold me when we hug.
I love how I get a feeling of protection
when I'm around you.
I love how everything is perfect.
I love how you see the person I really am,
yet you still want me.
I love how you have a passion for us
and you want to grow in your relationship.
I love how you make me cry,
but not because I'm upset or sad,
or you hurt me,
but because you make me the happiest
I've ever been.
I love waking up and talking to you.

I love how I anticipate seeing you.
I love how I get nervous when I see you,
but feel more comfortable with you
then I do with anyone else.
I love how you deal with my random thoughts and craziness.
I love how you insist everything will be alright,
and make me feel at ease.
I love how you give me weird looks
at awkward moments.
I love how I'm important to you.
I love how I'm your first choice.
I love how I make you happy.
I love how you make ME happy.
I love how I worry about you
and the dumb stuff you do.
I love how I only want to be with you.
I love how I constantly think about you.
I love when you get mad when someone says
something to upset me.
I love how just one smile from you can make
my entire mood change.
I love how I'm yours.
I just love...us.
I love everything about you.

She'd stroll through the village,

eyes fixed on the ground.
When greeted, the girl scarcely uttered a sound.
Since her parents death
a few years back,
she's lived on her own
in no more than a shack.
Her hair as red
as the fire of hell,
In the thoughts of men. her innocence fell.
They'd follow her in
the light of day,
besot by her
peculiar way.
They'd leave their wives in the dark of night,
to spy as she danced
beneath the moonlight.
One woman swore by God that she witnessed,
her reading a book of magic so wicked.
No wonder her husband held such foolish notions.
Possessed by this witch and all her love potions.
When questioned, the girl, she could not tell,
what power had she,
if not by spell; Could take hold of a man,
lead him into temptation, if not by witchcraft
or some incantation. Her persuasion rooted
in evil they deemed. Her protest heard
by way of her screams.

When they put her inside the old metal pot,
it's with the will of the devil himself that she fought.
It was said her fate would be redeemed,
if her body stayed below surface.
Named pure again in the eyes of God by
those who stood to bear witness.
Fully submerged,
She struggled for air, Sinking,
the angel with fire for hair.
With bibles in hand, they gathered around
Together they shouted while watching her drown.
Redemption then granted,
her sins pronounced clean,
by the men who condemned her,
to death, at sixteen.

3. the memories and fables

warning: vintage fairy tales,
fables & excerpts from faded memories

The Troll Wedding

One summer, a long, long time ago, the folk of Melbustad went up to the hill pastures with their herd. But they had been there only a short time when the cattle began to grow so restless that it was impossible to keep them in order. A number of different maidens tried to manage them, but without avail; until one came who was betrothed, and whose betrothal had but recently been celebrated. Then the cattle suddenly quieted down, and were easy to handle. So the maiden remained alone in the hills with no other company than a dog. And one afternoon as she sat in the hut, it seemed to her that her sweetheart came, sat down beside her, and began to talk about their getting married at once. But she sat still and made no reply, for she noticed a strangeness about him. By and by, more and more people came in, and they began to cover the table with silverware, and bring on dishes, and the bridesmaids brought the bridal crown, and the ornaments, and a handsome bridal gown, and they dressed her and put the crown on her head, as was the custom in those days, and they put rings on her hands.

And it seemed to her as though she knew all the people who were there; they were the women of the village, and the girls of her own age. But the dog was well aware that there was something uncanny about it all. He made his way down to Melbustad in flying leaps, and howled and barked in the most lamentable manner, and gave the people no rest until they followed him. The young fellow who was to marry the girl took his gun, and climbed the hills; and when he drew near, there stood a number of horses around the hut, saddled and bridled. He crept up to the hut, looked through a loophole in the wall, and saw a whole company sitting together inside. It was quite evident that they were trolls, the people from underground, and therefore he discharged his gun over the roof. At that moment the doors flew open, and a number of balls of gray yarn, one larger than the other, came shooting out about his legs. When he went in, there sat the maiden in her bridal finery, and nothing was missing but the ring on her little finger, then all would have been complete.

"In heaven's name, what has happened here?" he asked, as he looked around. All the silverware was still on the table, but all the tasty dishes had turned to moss and toadstools, and frogs and toads and the like.

"What does it all mean?" said he. "You are sitting here in all your glory, just like a bride?"

"How can you ask me?" answered the maiden. "You have been sitting here yourself, and talking about our wedding the whole

afternoon!"
"No, I have just come," said he. "It must have been some one else who had taken my shape!"
Then she gradually came to her senses; but not until long afterward was she altogether herself, and she told how she had firmly believed that her sweetheart himself, and all their friends and relatives had been there. He took her straight back to the village with him, and so that they need fear no such deviltry in the future, they celebrated their wedding while she was still clad in the bridal outfit of the underground folk. The crown and all the ornaments were hung up in Melbustad and it is said that they hang there to this very day.

In the land of Annam there once dwelt a man named Su, who sailed the seas as a merchant. Once his ship was suddenly driven on a distant shore by a great storm. It was a land of hills broken by ravines and green with luxuriant foliage, yet he could see something along the hills which looked like human dwellings. So he took some food with him and went ashore. No sooner had he entered the hills than he could see at either hand the entrances to caves, one close beside the other, like a row of beehives. So he stopped and looked into one of the openings. And in it sat two ogres, with teeth like spears and eyes like fiery lamps. They were just devouring a deer. The merchant was terrified by this sight and turned to flee; but the ogres had already noticed him and they caught him and dragged him into their cave. Then they talked to each other with animal sounds, and were about to tear his clothes from his body and devour him. But the merchant hurriedly took a bag of bread and dried meat out and offered it to them. They divided it, ate it up and it seemed to taste good to them. Then they once more went through the bag; but he gestured with his hand to show them that he had no more.

Then he said: "Let me go! Aboard my ship I have frying-pans and cooking-pots, vinegar and spices. With these I could prepare your food."

The ogres did not understand what he was saying, however, and were still ferocious. So he tried to make them understand in dumb show, and finally they seemed to get an idea of his meaning. So they went to the ship with him, and he brought his cooking gear to the cave, collected brush-wood, made a fire and cooked the remains of the deer. When it was done to a turn he gave them some of it to eat, and the two creatures devoured it with the greatest satisfaction. Then they left the cave and closed the opening with a great rock. In a short space of time they returned with another deer they had caught. The merchant skinned it, fetched fresh water, washed the meat and cooked several kettles full of it. Suddenly in came a whole herd of ogres, who devoured all he had cooked, and became quite animated over their eating. They all kept pointing to the kettle which seemed too small to them. When three or four days had passed, one of the ogres dragged in an enormous cooking-pot on his back, which was thenceforth used exclusively.

Now the ogres crowded about the merchant, bringing him wolves and deer and antelopes, which he had to cook for them, and when the meat was done they would call him to eat it with them.

Thus a few weeks passed and they gradually came to have such confidence in him that they let him run about freely. And the merchant listened to the sounds which they uttered, and learned to understand them. In fact, before very long he was able to speak the language of the ogres himself. This pleased the latter greatly, and they introduced him to a young ogre girl and made her his wife. She gave him valuables and fruit to win his confidence, and in course of time they grew much attached to each other.

One day the ogres all rose very early, and each one of them hung a string of radiant pearls about his neck. They ordered the merchant to be sure and cook a great quantity of meat. The merchant asked his wife what it all meant.

"This will be a day of high festival," answered she, "we have invited the great king to a banquet."

But to the other ogres she said: "The merchant has no string of pearls!"

Then each of the ogres gave him five pearls and his wife added ten, so that he had fifty pearls in all. These his wife threaded and hung the pearl necklace about his neck, and there was not one of the pearls which was not worth at least several hundred ounces of silver.

Then the merchant cooked the meat, and having done so left the cave with the whole herd in order to receive the great king. They came to a broad cave, in the middle of which stood a huge block of stone, as smooth and even as a table. Round it were stone seats. The place of honor was covered with a leopard-skin, and the rest of the seats with deerskins. Several dozen ogres were sitting around the cave in rank and file.

Suddenly a tremendous storm blew up, whirling around the dust in columns, and a monster appeared who had the figure of an ogre. The ogres all crowded out of the cave in a high state of excitement to receive him. The great king ran into the cave, sat down with his legs outstretched, and glanced about him with eyes as round as an eagle's. The whole herd followed him into the cave, and stood at either hand of him, looking up to him and folding their arms across their breasts in the form of a cross in order to do him honor.

The great king nodded, looked around and asked: "Are all the folk of the Wo-Me hills present?"

The entire herd declared that they were.

Then he saw the merchant and asked: "From whence does he hail?"

His wife answered for him, and all spoke with praise of his art as a cook. A couple of ogres brought in the cooked meat and spread it out on the table. Then the great king ate of it till he could eat no more, praised it with his mouth full, and said that in the future they were always to furnish him with food of this kind.

Then he looked at the merchant and asked: "Why is your necklace so short?"

With these words he took ten pearls from his own necklace, pearls as large and round as bullets of a blunderbuss. The merchant's wife quickly took them on his behalf and hung them around his neck; and the merchant crossed his arms like the ogres and spoke his thanks. Then the great king went off again, flying away like lightning on the storm.

In the course of time heaven sent the merchant children, two boys and a girl. They all had a human form and did not resemble their mother. Gradually the children learned to speak and their father taught them the language of men. They grew up, and were soon so strong that they could run across the hills as though on level ground.

One day the merchant's wife had gone out with one of the boys and the girl and had been absent for half-a-day. The north wind was blowing briskly, and in the merchant's heart there awoke a longing for his old home. He took his son by the hand and went down to the sea-shore. There his old ship was still lying, so he climbed into it with his boy, and in a day and a night was back in Annam again.

When he reached home he loosened two of his pearls from his chain, and sold them for a great quantity of gold, so that he could keep house in handsome style. He gave his son the name of Panther, and when the boy was fourteen years of age he could lift thirty hundred weight with ease. Yet he was rough by nature and fond of fighting. The general of Annam, astonished at his bravery, appointed him a colonel, and in putting down a revolt his services were so meritorious that he was already a general of the second rank when but eighteen.

At about this time another merchant was also driven ashore by a storm on the island of Wo-Me. When he reached land he saw a youth who asked him with astonishment: "Are you not from the Middle Kingdom?"

The merchant told him how he had come to be driven ashore on the island, and the youth led him to a little cave in a secret valley. Then he brought deer-flesh for him to eat, and talked with him. He told him that his father had also come from Annam, and it turned out that his father was an old acquaintance of the man to whom he was talking.

"We will have to wait until the wind blows from the North," said the youth, "then I will come and escort you. And I will give you a message of greeting to take to my father and brother."

"Why do you not go along yourself and hunt up your father?" asked the merchant.

"My mother does not come from the Middle Kingdom," replied the youth. "She is different in speech and appearance, so it cannot well be."

One day the wind blew strongly from the North, and the youth came and escorted the merchant to his ship, and ordered him, at parting, not to forget a single one of his words.

When the merchant returned to Annam, he went to the palace of Panther, the general, and told him all that had happened. When Panther listened to him telling about his brother, he sobbed with bitter grief. Then he secured leave of absence and sailed out to sea with two soldiers. Suddenly a typhoon arose, which lashed the waves until they spurted sky-high. The ship turned turtle, and Panther fell into the sea. He was seized by a creature and flung up on a strand where there seemed to be dwellings. The creature who had seized him looked like an ogre, so Panther addressed him in the ogre tongue. The ogre, surprised, asked him who he was, and Panther told him his whole story.

The ogre was pleased and said: "Wo-Me is my old home, but it lies about eight thousand miles away from here. This is the kingdom of the poison dragons."

Then the ogre fetched a ship and had Panther seat himself in it, while he himself pushed the ship before him through the water so that it clove the waves like an arrow. It took a whole night, but in the morning a shoreline appeared to the North, and there on the strand stood a youth on look-out. Panther recognized his brother. He stepped ashore and they clasped hands and wept. Then Panther turned around to thank the ogre, but the latter had already disappeared.

Panther now asked after his mother and sister and was told that both were well and happy, so he wanted to go to them with his brother. But the latter told him to wait, and went off alone. Not long after he came back with their mother and sister. And when they saw Panther, both wept with emotion. Panther now begged them to return with him to Annam.

But his mother replied: "I fear that if I went, people would mock me because of my figure."

"I am a high officer," replied Panther, "and people would not dare to insult you."

So they all went down to the ship together with him. A favorable wind filled their sails and they sped home swiftly as an arrow flies. On the third day they reached land. But the people whom they encountered were all seized with terror and ran away. Then Panther took off his mantle and divided it among the three so that they could dress themselves.

When they reached home and the mother saw her husband again, she at once began to scold him violently because he had said not a word to her when he went away. The members of his family, who all came to greet the wife of the master of the house, did so with fear and trembling. But Panther advised his mother to learn the language of the Middle Kingdom, dress in silks, and accustom herself to human food. This she agreed to do; yet she and her daughter had men's clothing made for them. The brother and sister gradually grew more fair of complexion, and looked like the people of the Middle Kingdom. Panther's brother was named Leopard, and his sister Ogrechild. Both possessed great bodily strength.

But Panther was not pleased to think that his brother was so uneducated, so he had him study. Leopard was highly gifted; he understood a book at first reading; yet he felt no inclination to become a man of learning. To shoot and to ride was what he best loved to do. So he rose to high rank as a professional soldier, and finally married the daughter of a distinguished official.

It was long before Ogrechild found a husband, because all suitors were afraid of their mother-in-law to be. But Ogrechild finally married one of her brother's subordinates. She could draw the strongest bow, and strike the tiniest bird at a distance of a hundred paces. Her arrow never fell to earth without having scored a hit. When her husband went out to battle she always accompanied him, and that he finally became a general was largely due to her. Leopard was already a field marshal at the age of thirty, and his mother accompanied him on his campaigns. When a dangerous enemy drew near, she buckled on armor, and took a knife in her hand to meet him in place of her son. And among the enemies who encountered her there was not a single one who did not flee from her in terror. Because of her courage the emperor bestowed upon her the title of "The Superwoman."

The Kingdom of Orges

Long, long ago, there once lived a king and a queen who had a daughter. One day, when the daughter went walking in the garden, a tremendous storm suddenly came up and carried her away with it. Now the storm had come from the bird with nine heads, who had robbed the princess, and brought her to his cave. The king did not know whither his daughter had disappeared, so he had proclaimed throughout the land: "Whoever brings back the princess may have her for his bride!"

Now a youth had seen the bird as he was carrying the princess to his cave. This cave, though, was in the middle of a sheer wall of rock. One could not climb up to it from below, nor could one climb down to it from above. And as the youth was walking around the rock, another youth came along and asked him what he was doing there. So the first youth told him that the bird with nine heads had carried off the king's daughter, and had brought her up to his cave. The other chap knew what he had to do. He called together his friends, and they lowered the youth to the cave in a basket. And when he went into the cave, he saw the king's daughter sitting there, and washing the wound of the bird with nine heads; for the hound of heaven had bitten off his tenth head, and his wound was still bleeding. The princess, however, motioned to the youth to hide, and he did so. When the king's daughter had washed his wound and bandaged it, the bird with nine heads felt so comfortable, that one after another, all his nine heads fell asleep. Then the youth stepped forth from his hiding-place, and cut off his nine heads with a sword. But the king's daughter said: "It would be best if you were hauled up first, and I came after."

"No," said the youth. "I will wait below here, until you are in safety." At first the king's daughter was not willing; yet at last she allowed herself to be persuaded, and climbed into the basket. But before she did so, she took a long pin from her hair, broke it into two halves and gave him one and kept the other. She also divided her silken kerchief with him, and told him to take good care of both her gifts. But when the other man had drawn up the king's daughter, he took her along with him, and left the youth in the cave, in spite of all his calling and pleading.

The youth now took a walk about the cave. There he saw a number of maidens, all of whom had been carried off by the bird with nine heads, and who had perished there of hunger. And on the wall hung a fish, nailed against it with four nails. When he touched the fish, the latter turned into a handsome youth, who thanked him for delivering him, and they agreed to regard each other as brothers. Soon the first youth grew very hungry. He stepped out in front of the cave to search for food, but only stones were lying there. Then, suddenly, he saw a great dragon, who was licking a stone. The youth imitated him, and before long his hunger had disappeared. He next asked the dragon how he could get away from the cave, and the dragon nodded his head in the direction of his tail, as much as to say he should seat himself upon it. So he climbed up, and in the twinkling of an eye he was down on the ground, and the dragon had disappeared. He then went on until he found a tortoise-shell full of beautiful pearls. But they were magic pearls, for if you flung them into the fire, the fire ceased to burn and if you flung them into the water, the water divided and you could walk through the midst of it. The youth took the pearls out of the tortoise-shell, and put them in his pocket. Not long after he reached the sea-shore. Here he flung a pearl into the sea, and at once the waters divided and he could see the sea-dragon. The sea-dragon cried: "Who is disturbing me here in my own kingdom?" The youth answered: "I found pearls in a tortoise-shell, and have flung one into the sea, and now the waters have divided for me."

"If that is the case," said the dragon, "then come into the sea with me and we will live there together." Then the youth recognized him for the same dragon whom he had seen in the cave. And with him was the youth with whom he had formed a bond of brotherhood: He was the dragon's son.

"Since you have saved my son and become his brother, I am your father," said the old dragon. And he entertained him hospitably with food and wine.

One day his friend said to him: "My father is sure to want to reward you. But accept no money, nor any jewels from him, but only the little gourd flask over yonder. With it you can conjure up whatever you wish."

And, sure enough, the old dragon asked him what he wanted by way of a reward, and the youth answered: "I want no money, nor any jewels. All I want is the little gourd flask over yonder."

At first the dragon did not wish to give it up, but at last he did let him have it, after all. And then the youth left the dragon's castle.

When he set his foot on dry land again he felt hungry. At once a table stood before him, covered with a fine and plenteous meal. He ate and drank. After he had gone on a while, he felt weary. And there stood an ass, waiting for him, on which he mounted. After he had ridden for a while, the ass's gait seemed too uneven, and along came a wagon, into which he climbed. But the wagon shook him up too, greatly, and he thought: "If I only had a litter! That would suit me better." No more had he thought so, than the litter came along, and he seated himself in it. And the bearers carried him to the city in which dwelt the king, the queen and their daughter.

When the other youth had brought back the king's daughter, it was decided to hold the wedding. But the king's daughter was not willing, and said: "He is not the right man. My deliverer will come and bring with him half of the long pin for my hair, and half my silken kerchief as a token." But when the youth did not appear for so long a time, and the other one pressed the king, the king grew impatient and said: "The wedding shall take place to-morrow!" Then the king's daughter went sadly through the streets of the city, and searched and searched in the hope of finding her deliverer. And this was on the very day that the litter arrived. The king's daughter saw the half of her silken handkerchief in the youth's hand, and filled with joy, she led him to her father. There he had to show his half of the long pin, which fitted the other exactly, and then the king was convinced that he was the right, true deliverer. The false bridegroom was now punished, the wedding celebrated, and they lived in peace and happiness till the end of their days.

The bird with nine heads

Long, long ago, there once lived a king and a queen who had a daughter. One day, when the daughter went walking in the garden, a tremendous storm suddenly came up and carried her away with it. Now the storm had come from the bird with nine heads, who had robbed the princess, and brought her to his cave. The king did not know whither his daughter had disappeared, so he had proclaimed throughout the land: "Whoever brings back the princess may have her for his bride!"

Now a youth had seen the bird as he was carrying the princess to his cave. This cave, though, was in the middle of a sheer wall of rock. One could not climb up to it from below, nor could one climb down to it from above. And as the youth was walking around the rock, another youth came along and asked him what he was doing there. So the first youth told him that the bird with nine heads had carried off the king's daughter, and had brought her up to his cave. The other chap knew what he had to do. He called together his friends, and they lowered the youth to the cave in a basket. And when he went into the cave, he saw the king's daughter sitting there, and washing the wound of the bird with nine heads; for the hound of heaven had bitten off his tenth head, and his wound was still bleeding. The princess, however, motioned to the youth to hide, and he did so. When the king's daughter had washed his wound and bandaged it, the bird with nine heads felt so comfortable, that one after another, all his nine heads fell asleep. Then the youth stepped forth from his hiding-place, and cut off his nine heads with a sword. But the king's daughter said: "It would be best if you were hauled up first, and I came after."

"No," said the youth. "I will wait below here, until you are in safety." At first the king's daughter was not willing; yet at last she allowed herself to be persuaded, and climbed into the basket. But before she did so, she took a long pin from her hair, broke it into two halves and gave him one and kept the other. She also divided her silken kerchief with him, and told him to take good care of both her gifts. But when the other man had drawn up the king's daughter, he took her along with him, and left the youth in the cave, in spite of all his calling and pleading.

The youth now took a walk about the cave. There he saw a number of maidens, all of whom had been carried off by the bird with nine heads, and who had perished there of hunger. And on the wall hung a fish, nailed against it with four nails. When he touched the fish, the latter turned into a handsome youth, who thanked him for delivering him, and they agreed to regard each other as brothers. Soon the first youth grew very hungry. He stepped out in front of the cave to search for food, but only stones were lying there. Then, suddenly, he saw a great dragon, who was licking a stone. The youth imitated him, and before long his hunger had disappeared. He next asked the dragon how he could get away from the cave, and the dragon nodded his head in the direction of his tail, as much as to say he should seat himself upon it. So he climbed up, and in the twinkling of an eye he was down on the ground, and the dragon had disappeared. He then went on until he found a tortoise-shell full of beautiful pearls. But they were magic pearls, for if you flung them into the fire, the fire ceased to burn and if you flung them into the water, the water divided and you could walk through the midst of it. The youth took the pearls out of the tortoise-shell, and put them in his pocket. Not long after he reached the sea-shore. Here he flung a pearl into the sea, and at once the waters divided and he could see the sea-dragon. The sea-dragon cried: "Who is disturbing me here in my own kingdom?" The youth answered: "I found pearls in a tortoise-shell, and have flung one into the sea, and now the waters have divided for me."

"If that is the case," said the dragon, "then come into the sea with me and we will live there together." Then the youth recognized him for the same dragon whom he had seen in the cave. And with him was the youth with whom he had formed a bond of brotherhood: He was the dragon's son.

"Since you have saved my son and become his brother, I am your father," said the old dragon. And he entertained him hospitably with food and wine.

One day his friend said to him: "My father is sure to want to reward you. But accept no money, nor any jewels from him, but only the little gourd flask over yonder. With it you can conjure up whatever you wish."

And, sure enough, the old dragon asked him what he wanted by way of a reward, and the youth answered: "I want no money, nor any jewels. All I want is the little gourd flask over yonder."

At first the dragon did not wish to give it up, but at last he did let him have it, after all. And then the youth left the dragon's castle.

When he set his foot on dry land again he felt hungry. At once a table stood before him, covered with a fine and plenteous meal. He ate and drank. After he had gone on a while, he felt weary. And there stood an ass, waiting for him, on which he mounted. After he had ridden for a while, the ass's gait seemed too uneven, and along came a wagon, into which he climbed. But the wagon shook him up too, greatly, and he thought: "If I only had a litter! That would suit me better." No more had he thought so, than the litter came along, and he seated himself in it. And the bearers carried him to the city in which dwelt the king, the queen and their daughter.

When the other youth had brought back the king's daughter, it was decided to hold the wedding. But the king's daughter was not willing, and said: "He is not the right man. My deliverer will come and bring with him half of the long pin for my hair, and half my silken kerchief as a token." But when the youth did not appear for so long a time, and the other one pressed the king, the king grew impatient and said: "The wedding shall take place to-morrow!" Then the king's daughter went sadly through the streets of the city, and searched and searched in the hope of finding her deliverer. And this was on the very day that the litter arrived. The king's daughter saw the half of her silken handkerchief in the youth's hand, and filled with joy, she led him to her father. There he had to show his half of the long pin, which fitted the other exactly, and then the king was convinced that he was the right, true deliverer. The false bridegroom was now punished, the wedding celebrated, and they lived in peace and happiness till the end of their days.

The star wife

In the days when the buffalo raced and thundered over the earth and the stars danced and sang in the sky, a brave young hunter lived on the bank of Battle River. He was fond of the red flowers and the blue sky; and when the rest of the Indians went out to hunt in waistcloths of skin he put on his fringed leggings all heavy with blue beads, and painted red rings and stripes on his face, till he was as gay as the earth and the sky himself. High-feather was his name, and he always wore a red swan's feather on his head.

One day, when High-feather was out with his bow and arrows, he came on a little beaten trail that he had never seen before, and he followed it—but he found that it went round and round and brought him back to where he had started. It came from nowhere, and it went to nowhere.

"What sort of animal has made this?" he said. And he lay down in the middle of the ring to think, looking up into the blue sky.

While he lay thinking, he saw a little speck up above him in the sky, and thought it was an eagle. But the speck grew bigger, and sank down and down, till he saw it was a great basket coming down out of the sky. He jumped up and ran back to a little hollow and lay down to hide in a patch of tall red flowers. Then he peeped out and saw the basket come down to the earth and rest on the grass in the middle of the ring. Twelve beautiful maidens were leaning over the edge of the basket. They were not Indian maidens, for their faces were pink and white, and their long hair was bright red-brown like a fox's fur, and their clothes were sky-blue and floating light as cobwebs.

The maidens jumped out of the basket and began to dance round and round the ring-trail, one behind the other, drumming with their fingers on little drums of eagle-skin, and singing such beautiful songs as High-feather had never heard. Then High-feather jumped up and ran towards the ring, crying out, "Let me dance and sing with you!"

The maidens were frightened, and ran to the basket and jumped in, and the basket flew up into the sky, and grew smaller till at last he could not see it at all.

The young man went home to his wigwam, and his mother roasted buffalo meat for his dinner; but he could not eat, and he could not think of anything but the twelve beautiful maidens. His mother begged him to tell her what the matter was; and at last he told her, and said he would never be happy till he brought one of the maidens home to be his wife.

"Those must be the Star-people," said his mother, who was a great magician—the prairie was full of magic in those days, before the white man came and the buffalo went. "You had better take an Indian girl for your wife. Don't think any more of the Star-maidens, or you will have much trouble."

"I care little how much trouble I have, so long as I get a Star-maiden for my wife," he said; "and I am going to get one, if I have to wait till the world ends."

"If you must, you must," said his mother.

So next morning she sewed a bit of gopher's fur on to his feather; and he ate a good breakfast of buffalo meat and tramped away over the prairie to the dancing ring. As soon as he came into the ring he turned into a gopher; but there were no gophers' holes there for him to hide in, so he had to lie in the grass and wait.

Presently he saw a speck up in the sky, and the speck grew larger and larger till it became a basket, and the basket came down and down till it rested on the earth in the middle of the ring.

The eldest maiden put her head over the edge and looked all around, north and east and south and west.

"There is no man here," she said. So they all jumped out to have their dance. But before they came to the beaten ring the youngest maiden spied the gopher, and called out to her sisters to look at it.

"Away! away!" cried the eldest maiden. "No gopher would dare to come on our dancing ground. It is a conjuror in disguise!"

So she took her youngest sister by the arm and pulled her away to the basket, and they all jumped in and the basket went sailing up into the sky before High-feather could get out of his gopher skin or say a word.

The young man went home very miserable; but when his mother heard what had happened she said: "It is a hard thing you want to do; but if you must, you must. To-night I will make some fresh magic, and you can try again to-morrow."

Next morning High-feather asked for his breakfast; but his mother said, "You must not have any buffalo meat, or it will spoil the magic. You must not eat anything but the wild strawberries you find on the prairie as you go."

Then she sewed a little bit of a mouse's whisker on to his red feather; and he tramped away across the prairie, picking wild strawberries and eating them as he went, till he came to the dancing ring. As soon as he was inside the ring he turned into a little mouse, and made friends with the family of mice that lived in a hole under the grass; and the mother mouse promised to help him all she could.

They had not waited long when the basket came dropping down out of the sky. The eldest sister put her head over the edge, and looked all around, north and west and south and east and down on the ground.

"There is no man here," she said, "and I do not see any gopher; but you must be very careful."

So they all got out of the basket, and began to dance round the ring, drumming and singing as they went. But when they came near the mouse's nest the eldest sister held up her hand, and they stopped dancing and held their breath. Then she tapped on the ground and listened.

"It does not sound so hollow as it did," she said, "The mice have a visitor."

And she tapped again, and called out, "Come and show yourselves, you little traitors, or we will dig you up!"

But the mother mouse had made another door to her nest, just outside the ring, working very fast with all her toes; and while the maidens were looking for her inside the ring she came out at the other door with all her children and scampered away across the prairie.

The maidens turned round and ran after them; all but the youngest sister, who did not want any one to be killed; and High-feather came out of the hole and turned himself into what he was, and caught her by the arm.

"Come home and marry me," he said, "and dance with the Indian maidens; and I will hunt for you, and my mother will cook for you, and you will be much happier than up in the sky."

Her sisters came rushing round her, and begged her to go back home to the sky with them; but she looked into the young man's eyes, and said she would go with him wherever he went. So the other maidens went weeping and wailing up into the sky, and High-feather took his Star-wife home to his tent on the bank of the Battle River.

High-feather's mother was glad to see them both; but she whispered in his ear: "You must never let her out of your sight if you want to keep her; you must take her with you everywhere you go."

And he did so. He took her with him every time he went hunting, and he made her a bow and arrows, but she would never use them; she would pick wild strawberries and gooseberries and raspberries as they went along, but she would never kill anything; and she would never eat anything that any one else had killed. She only ate berries and crushed corn.

One day, while the young man's wife was embroidering feather stars on a dancing-cloth, and his mother was gossiping in a tent at the end of the village, a little yellow bird flew in and perched on High-feather's shoulder, and whispered in his ear:

"There is a great flock of wild red swans just over on Loon Lake. If you come quickly and quietly you can catch them before they fly away; but do not tell your wife, for red swans cannot bear the sight of a woman, and they can tell if one comes within a mile of them."

High-feather had never seen or heard of a red swan before; all the red feathers he wore he had had to paint. He looked at his wife, and as she was sewing busily and looking down at her star embroidering he thought he could slip away and get back before she knew he had gone. But as soon as he was out of sight the little yellow bird flew in and perched on her shoulder, and sang her such a beautiful song about her sisters in the sky that she forgot everything else and slipped out and ran like the wind, and got to the dancing ring just as her sisters came down in their basket. Then they all gathered round her, and begged her to go home with them.

But she only said, "High-feather is a brave man, and he is very good to me, and I will never leave him."

When they saw they could not make her leave her husband, the eldest sister said: "If you must stay, you must. But just come up for an hour, to let your father see you, because he has been mourning for you ever since you went away."

The Star-wife did not wish to go, but she wanted to see her father once more, so she got into the basket and it sailed away up into the sky. Her father was very glad to see her, and she was very glad to see him, and they talked and they talked till the blue sky was getting gray. Then she remembered that she ought to have gone home long before.

"Now I must go back to my husband," she said.

"That you shall never do!" said her father.

And he shut her up in a white cloud and said she should stay there till she promised never to go back to the prairie. She begged to be let out, but it was no use.

Then she began to weep; and she wept so much that the cloud began to weep too, and it was weeping itself quite away. So her father saw she would go down to the earth in rain if he kept her in the cloud any longer, and he let her out.

"What must I do for you," he said, "to make you stay with us here and be happy?"

"I will not stay here," she said, "unless my husband comes and lives here too."

"I will send for him at once," said her father. So he sent the basket down empty, and it rested in the middle of the dancing ring.

Now when High-feather reached Loon Lake he found it covered with red swans. He shot two with one arrow, and then all the rest flew away. He picked up the two swans and hurried back to his tent, and there lay the dancing-cloth with the feather stars on it half finished, but no wife could he see. He called her, but she did not answer. He rushed out, with the two red swans still slung round his neck and hanging down his back, and ran to the dancing ring, but nobody was there.

"I will wait till she comes back," he said to himself, "if I have to wait till the world ends." So he threw himself down on the grass and lay looking up at the stars till he went to sleep.

Early in the morning he heard a rustling on the grass, and when he opened his eyes he saw the great basket close beside him. He jumped up, with the two red swans still slung round his neck, and climbed into the basket. There was nobody there; and when he began to climb out again he found that the basket was half way up to the sky. It went up and up, and at last it came into the Star-country, where his wife was waiting for him. Her father gave them a beautiful blue tent to live in, and High-feather was happy enough for a while; but he soon grew tired of the cloud-berries that the Star-people ate, and he longed to tramp over the solid green prairie, so he asked his wife's father to let him take her back to the earth.

"No," said the Star-man, "because then I should never see her again. If you stay with us you will soon forget the dull old earth."

The young man said nothing; but he put on the wings of one of the red swans, and he put the other red swan's wings on his wife, and they leapt over the edge of the Star-country and flew down through the air to the prairie, and came to the tent where High-feather's mother was mourning for them; and there was a great feast in the village because they had come back safe and sound.

The Star-wife finished embroidering her dancing-cloth that day; and whenever the Indians danced she danced with them. She never went back to the Star-maidens' dancing ring; but she still lived on berries and corn, because she would never kill anything,—except one thing, and that was the little yellow bird. It flew into the tent one day when High-feather had his back turned, and began to whisper into the Star-wife's ear; but it never came to trouble her again

The maiden who loved a fish

There was once among the Marshpees, a small tribe who have their hunting-grounds on the shores of the Great Lake, near the Cape of Storms, a woman whose name was Awashanks. She was rather silly and very idle. For days together she would sit doing nothing. Then she was so ugly and ill-shaped that not one of the youths of the village would have aught to say to her by way of courtship or marriage. She squinted very much; her face was long and thin, her nose excessively large and humped, her teeth crooked and projecting, her chin almost as sharp as the bill of a loon, and her ears as large as those of a deer. Altogether she was a very odd and strangely formed woman, and wherever she went she never failed to excite much laughter and derision among those who thought that ugliness and deformity were fit subjects for ridicule.

Though so very ugly, there was one faculty she possessed in a more remarkable degree than any woman of the tribe. It was that of singing. Nothing, unless such could be found in the land of spirits, could equal the sweetness of her voice or the beauty of her songs. Her favorite place of resort was a small hill, a little removed from the river of her people, and there, seated beneath the shady trees, she would while away the hours of summer with her charming songs. So beautiful and melodious were the things she uttered that, by the time she had sung a single sentence, the branches above her head would be filled with the birds that came thither to listen, the thickets around her would be crowded with beasts, and the waters rolling beside her would be alive with fishes, all attracted by the sweet sounds. From the minnow to the porpoise, from the wren to the eagle, from the snail to the lobster, from the mouse to the mole—all hastened to the spot to listen to the charming songs of the hideous Marshpee maiden.

Among the fishes which repaired every night to the vicinity of the Little Hillock, which was the chosen resting-place of the ugly songstress, was the great chief of the trouts, a tribe of fish inhabiting the river near by. The chief was of a far greater size than the people of his nation usually are, being as long as a man and quite as broad.

Of all the creatures which came to listen to the singing of Awashanks none appeared to enjoy it so highly as the chief of the trouts. As his bulk prevented him from approaching so near as he wished, he, from time to time, in his eagerness to enjoy the music to the best advantage, ran his nose into the ground, and thus worked his way a considerable distance into the land. Nightly he continued his exertions to approach the source of the delightful sounds he heard, till at length he had plowed out a wide and handsome channel, and so effected his passage from the river to the hill, a distance extending an arrow's-flight. Thither he repaired every night at the commencement of darkness, sure to meet the maiden who had become so necessary to his happiness.

Soon he began to speak of the pleasure he enjoyed, and to fill the ears of Awashanks with fond protestations of his love and affection. Instead of singing to him, she now began to listen to his voice. It was something so new and strange to her to hear the tones of love and courtship, a thing so unusual to be told she was beautiful, that it is not wonderful her head was turned by the new incident, and that she began to think the voice of her lover the sweetest she had ever heard.

Only one thing marred their happiness. This was that the trout could not live upon land, nor the maiden in the water. This state of things gave them much sorrow.

They had met one evening at the usual place, and were discoursing together, lamenting that two who loved each other so, should be doomed always to live apart, when a man appeared close to Awashanks. He asked the lovers why they seemed to be so sad.

The chief of the trouts told the stranger the cause of their sorrow.

"Be not grieved nor hopeless," said the stranger, when the chief had finished. "The impediments can be removed. I am the spirit who presides over fishes, and though I cannot make a man or woman of a fish, I can make them into fish. Under my power Awashanks shall become a beautiful trout."

With that he bade the girl follow him into the river. When they had waded in some little depth he took up some water in his hand and poured it on her head, muttering some words, of which none but himself knew the meaning. Immediately a change took place in her. Her body took the form of a fish, and in a few moments she was a complete trout.

Having accomplished this transformation the spirit gave her to the chief of the trouts, and the pair glided off into the deep and quiet waters. She did not, however, forget the land of her birth. Every season, on the same night as that upon which her disappearance from her tribe had been wrought, there were to be seen two trouts of enormous size playing in the water off the shore. They continued their visits till the palefaces came to the country, when, deeming themselves to be in danger from a people who paid no reverence to the spirits of the land, they bade it adieu forever.

The Queen Bee

Two kings' sons once upon a time went into the world to seek their fortunes; but they soon fell into a wasteful foolish way of living, so that they could not return home again. Then their brother, who was a dwarf, went out to seek for his brothers: but when he had found them they only laughed at him, to think that he, who was so young and simple, should try to travel through the world, when they, who were so much wiser, had been unable to get on. However, they all set out on their journey together, and came at last to an ant-hill. The two elder brothers would have pulled it down, in order to see how the poor ants in their fright would run about and carry off their eggs. But the dwarf said, 'Let the poor things enjoy themselves, I will not suffer you to trouble them.'

So on they went, and came to a lake where many many ducks were swimming about. The two brothers wanted to catch two, and roast them. But the dwarf said, 'Let the poor things enjoy themselves, you shall not kill them.' Next they came to a bees'-nest in a hollow tree, and there was so much honey that it ran down the trunk; and the two brothers wanted to light a fire under the tree and kill the bees, so as to get their honey. But the dwarf held them back, and said, 'Let the pretty insects enjoy themselves, I cannot let you burn them.'

At length the three brothers came to a castle: and as they passed by the stables they saw fine horses standing there, but all were of marble, and no man was to be seen. Then they went through all the rooms, till they came to a door on which were three locks: but in the middle of the door was a wicket, so that they could look into the next room. There they saw a little grey old man sitting at a table; and they called to him once or twice, but he did not hear: however, they called a third time, and then he rose and came out to them.

He said nothing, but took hold of them and led them to a beautiful table covered with all sorts of good things: and when they had eaten and drunk, he showed each of them to a bed-chamber.

The next morning he came to the eldest and took him to a marble table, where there were three tablets, containing an account of the means by which the castle might be disenchanted. The first tablet said: 'In the wood, under the moss, lie the thousand pearls belonging to the king's daughter; they must all be found: and if one be missing by set of sun, he who seeks them will be turned into marble.'

The eldest brother set out, and sought for the pearls the whole day: but the evening came, and he had not found the first hundred: so he was turned into stone as the tablet had foretold.

The next day the second brother undertook the task; but he succeeded no better than the first; for he could only find the second hundred of the pearls; and therefore he too was turned into stone.

At last came the dwarf's turn; and he looked in the moss; but it was so hard to find the pearls, and the job was so tiresome!—so he sat down upon a stone and cried. And as he sat there, the king of the ants (whose life he had saved) came to help him, with five thousand ants; and it was not long before they had found all the pearls and laid them in a heap.

The second tablet said: 'The key of the princess's bed-chamber must be fished up out of the lake.' And as the dwarf came to the brink of it, he saw the two ducks whose lives he had saved swimming about; and they dived down and soon brought in the key from the bottom.

The third task was the hardest. It was to choose out the youngest and the best of the king's three daughters. Now they were all beautiful, and all exactly alike: but he was told that the eldest had eaten a piece of sugar, the next some sweet syrup, and the youngest a spoonful of honey; so he was to guess which it was that had eaten the honey.

Then came the queen of the bees, who had been saved by the dwarf from the fire, and she tried the lips of all three; but at last she sat upon the lips of the one that had eaten the honey: and so the dwarf knew which was the youngest. Thus the spell was broken, and all who had been turned into stones awoke, and took their proper forms. And the dwarf married the youngest and the best of the princesses, and was king after her father's death; but his two brothers married the other two sisters.

The little elder tree mother

Once upon a time there was a little boy who had taken cold. He had gone out and got his feet wet; though nobody could imagine how it had happened, for it was quite dry weather. So his mother undressed him, put him to bed, and had the tea-pot brought in, to make him a good cup of Elderflower tea.

Just at that moment the merry old man came in who lived up a-top of the house all alone; for he had neither wife nor children—but he liked children very much, and knew so many fairy tales, that it was quite delightful.

"Now drink your tea," said the boy's mother; "then, perhaps, you may hear a fairy tale."

"If I had but something new to tell," said the old man. "But how did the child get his feet wet?"

"That is the very thing that nobody can make out," said his mother.

"Am I to hear a fairy tale?" asked the little boy.

"Yes, if you can tell me exactly—for I must know that first—how deep the gutter is in the little street opposite, that you pass through in going to school."

"Just up to the middle of my boot," said the child; "but then I must go into the deep hole."

"Ah, ah! That's where the wet feet came from," said the old man. "I ought now to tell you a story; but I don't know any more."

"You can make one in a moment," said the little boy. "My mother says that all you look at can be turned into a fairy tale: and that you can find a story in everything."

"Yes, but such tales and stories are good for nothing. The right sort come of themselves; they tap at my forehead and say, 'Here we are.'"

"Won't there be a tap soon?" asked the little boy. And his mother laughed, put some Elder-flowers in the tea-pot, and poured boiling water upon them.

"Do tell me something! Pray do!"

"Yes, if a fairy tale would come of its own accord; but they are proud and haughty, and come only when they choose. Stop!"

said he, all on a sudden. "I have it! Pay attention! There is one in the tea-pot!"

And the little boy looked at the tea-pot. The cover rose more and more; and the Elder-flowers came forth so fresh and white, and shot up long branches. Out of the spout even did they spread themselves on all sides, and grew larger and larger; it was a splendid Elderbush, a whole tree; and it reached into the very bed, and pushed the curtains aside. How it bloomed! And what an odour!

In the middle of the bush sat a friendly-looking old woman in a most strange dress. It was quite green, like the leaves of the elder, and was trimmed with large white Elder-flowers; so that at first one could not tell whether it was a stuff, or a natural green and real flowers.

"What's that woman's name?" asked the little boy.

"The Greeks and Romans," said the old man, "called her a Dryad; but that we do not understand. The people who live in Copenhagen have a much better name for her; they call her 'old Granny'—and she it is to whom you are to pay attention. Now listen, and look at the beautiful Elderbush.

"Just such another large blooming Elder Tree stands near Copenhagen. It grew there in the corner of a little miserable court-yard; and under it sat, of an afternoon, in the most splendid sunshine, two old people; an old, old seaman, and his old, old wife. They had great-grand-children, and were soon to celebrate the fiftieth anniversary of their marriage; but they could not exactly recollect the date: and old Granny sat in the tree, and looked as pleased as now.

"'I know the date,' said she; but those below did not hear her, for they were talking about old times.

"'Yes, can't you remember when we were very little,' said the old seaman, 'and ran and played about? It was the very same court-yard where we now are, and we stuck slips in the ground, and made a garden.'

"'I remember it well,' said the old woman; 'I remember it quite well. We watered the slips, and one of them was an Elderbush. It took root, put forth green shoots, and grew up to be the large tree under which we old folks are now sitting.'

"'To be sure,' said he. 'And there in the corner stood a waterpail, where I used to swim my boats.'

"'True; but first we went to school to learn somewhat,' said she; 'and then we were confirmed. We both cried; but in the afternoon we went up the Round Tower, and looked down on Copenhagen, and far, far away over the water; then we went to Friedericksberg, where the King and the Queen were sailing about in their splendid barges.'

"'But I had a different sort of sailing to that, later; and that, too, for many a year; a long way off, on great voyages.'

"'Yes, many a time have I wept for your sake,' said she. 'I thought you were dead and gone, and lying down in the deep waters. Many a night have I got up to see if the wind had not changed: and changed it had, sure enough; but you never came. I remember so well one day, when the rain was pouring down in torrents, the scavengers were before the house where I was in service, and I had come up with the dust, and remained standing at the door—it was dreadful weather—when just as I was there, the postman came and gave me a letter. It was from you! What a tour that letter had made! I opened it instantly and read: I laughed and wept. I was so happy. In it I read that you were in warm lands where the coffee-tree grows. What a blessed land that must be! You related so much, and I saw it all the while the rain was pouring down, and I standing there with the dust-box. At the same moment came someone who embraced me.'

"'Yes; but you gave him a good box on his ear that made it tingle!'

"'But I did not know it was you. You arrived as soon as your letter, and you were so handsome—that you still are—and had a long yellow silk handkerchief round your neck, and a bran new hat on; oh, you were so dashing! Good heavens! What weather it was, and what a state the street was in!'

"'And then we married,' said he. 'Don't you remember? And then we had our first little boy, and then Mary, and Nicholas, and Peter, and Christian.'

"'Yes, and how they all grew up to be honest people, and were beloved by everybody.'

"'And their children also have children,' said the old sailor; 'yes, those are our grand-children, full of strength and vigor. It was, methinks about this season that we had our wedding.'

"'Yes, this very day is the fiftieth anniversary of the marriage,' said old Granny, sticking her head between the two old people; who thought it was their neighbor who nodded to them. They looked at each other and held one another by the hand.

Soon after came their children, and their grand-children; for they knew well enough that it was the day of the fiftieth anniversary, and had come with their gratulations that very morning; but the old people had forgotten it, although they were able to remember all that had happened many years ago. And the Elderbush sent forth a strong odour in the sun, that was just about to set, and shone right in the old people's faces. They both looked so rosy-cheeked; and the youngest of the grandchildren danced around them, and called out quite delighted, that there was to be something very splendid that evening—they were all to have hot potatoes. And old Nanny nodded in the bush, and shouted 'hurrah!' with the rest."

"But that is no fairy tale," said the little boy, who was listening to the story.

"The thing is, you must understand it," said the narrator; "let us ask old Nanny."

"That was no fairy tale, 'tis true," said old Nanny; "but now it's coming. The most wonderful fairy tales grow out of that which is reality; were that not the case, you know, my magnificent Elderbush could not have grown out of the tea-pot."

And then she took the little boy out of bed, laid him on her bosom, and the branches of the Elder Tree, full of flowers, closed around her. They sat in an aerial dwelling, and it flew with them through the air. Oh, it was wondrous beautiful! Old Nanny had grown all of a sudden a young and pretty maiden; but her robe was still the same green stuff with white flowers, which she had worn before. On her bosom she had a real Elderflower, and in her yellow waving hair a wreath of the flowers; her eyes were so large and blue that it was a pleasure to look at them; she kissed the boy, and now they were of the same age and felt alike.

Hand in hand they went out of the bower, and they were standing in the beautiful garden of their home. Near the green lawn papa's walking-stick was tied, and for the little ones it seemed to be endowed with life; for as soon as they got astride it, the round polished knob was turned into a magnificent neighing head, a long black mane fluttered in the breeze, and four slender yet strong legs shot out. The animal was strong and handsome, and away they went at full gallop round the lawn.

"Huzza! Now we are riding miles off," said the boy. "We are riding away to the castle where we were last year!"

And on they rode round the grass-plot; and the little maiden, who, we know, was no one else but old Nanny, kept on crying out, "Now we are in the country! Don't you see the farm-house yonder? And there is an Elder Tree standing beside it; and the cock is scraping away the earth for the hens, look, how he struts! And now we are close to the church. It lies high upon the hill, between the large oak-trees, one of which is half decayed. And now we are by the smithy, where the fire is blazing, and where the half-naked men are banging with their hammers till the sparks fly about. Away! away! To the beautiful country-seat!"

And all that the little maiden, who sat behind on the stick, spoke of, flew by in reality. The boy saw it all, and yet they were only going round the grass-plot. Then they played in a side avenue, and marked out a little garden on the earth; and they took Elder-blossoms from their hair, planted them, and they grew just like those the old people planted when they were children, as related before. They went hand in hand, as the old people had done when they were children; but not to the Round Tower, or to Friedericksberg; no, the little damsel wound her arms round the boy, and then they flew far away through all Denmark. And spring came, and summer; and then it was autumn, and then winter; and a thousand pictures were reflected in the eye and in the heart of the boy; and the little girl always sang to him, "This you will never forget." And during their whole flight the Elder Tree smelt so sweet and odorous; he remarked the roses and the fresh beeches, but the Elder Tree had a more wondrous fragrance, for its flowers hung on the breast of the little maiden; and there, too, did he often lay his head during the flight.

"It is lovely here in spring!" said the young maiden. And they stood in a beech-wood that had just put on its first green, where the woodroof at their feet sent forth its fragrance, and the pale-red anemony looked so pretty among the verdure. "Oh, would it were always spring in the sweetly-smelling

Danish beech-forests!"

"It is lovely here in summer!" said she. And she flew past old castles of by-gone days of chivalry, where the red walls and the embattled gables were mirrored in the canal, where the swans were swimming, and peered up into the old cool avenues. In the fields the corn was waving like the sea; in the ditches red and yellow flowers were growing; while wild-drone flowers, and blooming convolvuluses were creeping in the hedges; and towards evening the moon rose round and large, and the haycocks in the meadows smelt so sweetly. "This one never forgets!"

"It is lovely here in autumn!" said the little maiden. And suddenly the atmosphere grew as blue again as before; the forest grew red, and green, and yellow-colored. The dogs came leaping along, and whole flocks of wild-fowl flew over the cairn, where blackberry-bushes were hanging round the old stones. The sea was dark blue, covered with ships full of white sails; and in the barn old women, maidens, and children were sitting picking hops into a large cask; the young sang songs, but the old told fairy tales of mountain-sprites and soothsayers. Nothing could be more charming.

"It is delightful here in winter!" said the little maiden. And all the trees were covered with hoar-frost; they looked like white corals; the snow crackled under foot, as if one had new boots on; and one falling star after the other was seen in the sky. The Christmas-tree was lighted in the room; presents were there, and good-humor reigned. In the country the violin sounded in the room of the peasant; the newly-baked cakes were attacked; even the poorest child said, "It is really delightful here in winter!"

Yes, it was delightful; and the little maiden showed the boy everything; and the Elder Tree still was fragrant, and the red flag, with the white cross, was still waving: the flag under which the old seaman in the New Booths had sailed. And the boy grew up to be a lad, and was to go forth in the wide world-far, far away to warm lands, where the coffee-tree grows; but at his departure the little maiden took an Elder-blossom from her bosom, and gave it him to keep; and it was placed between the leaves of his Prayer-Book; and when in foreign lands he opened the book, it was always at the place where the keepsake-flower lay; and the more he looked at it, the fresher it became; he felt as it were, the fragrance of the Danish groves; and from among the leaves of the flowers he could distinctly see the little maiden, peeping forth with her bright blue eyes—and then she whispered, "It is delightful here in Spring, Summer, Autumn, and Winter"; and a hundred visions glided before his mind.

Thus passed many years, and he was now an old man, and sat with his old wife under the blooming tree. They held each other by the hand, as the old grand-father and grand-mother yonder in Copenhagen did, and they talked exactly like them of old times, and of the fiftieth anniversary of their wedding.

The little maiden, with the blue eyes, and with Elder-blossoms in her hair, sat in the tree, nodded to both of them, and said,

"To-day is the fiftieth anniversary!"

And then she took two flowers out of her hair, and kissed them. First, they shone like silver, then like gold; and when they laid them on the heads of the old people, each flower became a golden crown. So there they both sat, like a king and a queen, under the fragrant tree, that looked exactly like an elder: the old man told his wife the story of "Old Nanny," as it had been told him when a boy. And it seemed to both of them it contained much that resembled their own history; and those parts that were like it pleased them best.

"Thus it is," said the little maiden in the tree, "some call me 'Old Nanny,' others a 'Dryad,' but, in reality, my name is 'Remembrance'; 'tis I who sit in the tree that grows and grows! I can remember; I can tell things! Let me see if you have my flower still?"

And the old man opened his Prayer-Book. There lay the Elder-blossom, as fresh as if it had been placed there but a short time before; and Remembrance nodded, and the old people, decked with crowns of gold, sat in the flush of the evening sun. They closed their eyes, and—and—! Yes, that's the end of the story!

The little boy lay in his bed; he did not know if he had dreamed or not, or if he had been listening while someone told him the story. The tea-pot was standing on the table, but no Elder Tree was growing out of it! And the old man, who had been talking, was just on the point of going out at the door, and he did go.

"How splendid that was!" said the little boy. "Mother, I have been to warm countries."

"So I should think," said his mother. "When one has drunk two good cupfuls of Elder-flower tea, 'tis likely enough one goes into warm climates"; and she tucked him up nicely, least he should take cold. "You have had a good sleep while I have been sitting here, and arguing with him whether it was a story or a fairy tale."

"And where is old Nanny?" asked the little boy.

"In the tea-pot," said his mother; "and there she may remain."

Prince darling

ONCE upon a time there lived a king who was so just and kind that his subjects called him "the Good King." It happened one day, when he was out hunting, that a little white rabbit, which his dogs were chasing, sprang into his arms for shelter. The King stroked it gently, and said to it:

"Well, bunny, as you have come to me for protection I will see that nobody hurts you."

And he took it home to his palace and had it put in a pretty little house, with all sorts of nice things to eat.

That night, when he was alone in his room, a beautiful lady suddenly appeared before him; her long dress was as white as snow, and she had a crown of white roses upon her head. The good King was very much surprised to see her, for he knew his door had been tightly shut, and he could not think how she had got in. But she said to him:

"I am the Fairy Truth. I was passing through the wood when you were out hunting, and I wished to find out if you were really good, as everybody said you were, so I took the shape of a little rabbit and came to your arms for shelter, for I know that those who are merciful to animals will be still kinder to their fellow-men. If you had refused to help me I should have been certain that you were wicked. I thank you for the kindness you have shown me, which has made me your friend for ever. You have only to ask me for anything you want and I promise that I will give it to you."

"Madam," said the good King, "since you are a fairy you no doubt know all my wishes. I have but one son whom I love very dearly, that is why he is called Prince Darling. If you are really good enough to wish to do me a favor, I beg that you will become his friend."

"With all my heart," answered the Fairy. "I can make your son the handsomest prince in the world, or the richest, or the most powerful; choose whichever you like for him."

"I do not ask either of these things for my son," replied the good King; "but if you will make him the best of princes, I shall indeed be grateful to you. What good would it do him to be rich, or handsome, or to possess all the kingdoms of the world if he were wicked? You know well he would still be unhappy. Only a good man can be really contented."

"You are quite right," answered the Fairy; "but it is not in my power to make Prince Darling a good man unless he will help me; he must himself try hard to become good, I can only promise to give him good advice, to scold him for his faults, and to punish him if he will not correct and punish himself."

The good King was quite satisfied with this promise; and very soon afterward he died.

Prince Darling was very sorry, for he loved his father with all his heart, and he would willingly have given all his kingdoms and all his treasures of gold and silver if they could have kept the good King with him.

Two days afterward, when the Prince had gone to bed, the Fairy suddenly appeared to him and said:

"I promised your father that I would be your friend, and to keep my word I have come to bring you a present." At the same time she put a little gold ring upon his finger.

"Take great care of this ring," she said: "it is more precious than diamonds; every time you do a bad deed it will prick your finger, but if, in spite of its pricking, you go on in your own evil way, you will lose my friendship, and I shall become your enemy."

So saying, the Fairy disappeared, leaving Prince Darling very much astonished.

For some time he behaved so well that the ring never pricked him, and that made him so contented that his subjects called him Prince Darling the Happy.

One day, however, he went out hunting, but could get no sport, which put him in a very bad temper; it seemed to him as he rode along that his ring was pressing into his finger, but as it did not prick him he did not heed it. When he got home and went to his own room, his little dog Bibi ran to meet him, jumping round him with pleasure. "Get away!" said the Prince, quite gruffly. "I don't want you, you are in the way."

The poor little dog, who didn't understand this at all, pulled at his coat to make him at least look at her, and this made Prince Darling so cross that he gave her quite a hard kick.

Instantly his ring pricked him sharply, as if it had been a pin. He was very much surprised, and sat down in a corner of his room feeling quite ashamed of himself.

"I believe the Fairy is laughing at me," he thought. "Surely I can have done no great wrong in just kicking a tiresome animal! What is the good of my being ruler of a great kingdom if I am not even allowed to do what I want?"

"I am not making fun of you," said a voice, answering Prince Darling's thoughts. "You have committed three faults. First of all, you were out of temper because you could not have what you wanted, and you thought all men and animals were only made to do your pleasure; then you were really angry, which is very naughty indeed; and lastly, you were cruel to a poor little animal who did not in the least deserve to be ill-treated.

"I know you are far above a little dog, but if it were right and allowable that great people should ill-treat all who are beneath them, I might at this moment beat you, or kill you, for a fairy is greater than a man. The advantage of possessing a great empire is not to be able to do the evil that one desires, but to do all the good that one possibly can."

The Prince saw how naughty he had been, and promised to try and do better in future, but he did not keep his word. The fact was he had been brought up by a foolish nurse, who had spoiled him when he was little. If he wanted anything he only had to cry and fret and stamp his feet and she would give him whatever he asked for, which had made him self-willed; also she had told him from morning to night that he would one day be a king, and that kings were very happy, because everyone was bound to obey and respect them, and no one could prevent them from doing just as they liked.

When the Prince grew old enough to understand, he soon learned that there could be nothing worse than to be proud, obstinate, and conceited, and he had really tried to cure himself of these defects, but by that time all his faults had become habits; and a bad habit is very hard to get rid of. Not that he was naturally of a bad disposition; he was truly sorry when he had been naughty, and said:

"I am very unhappy to have to struggle against my anger and pride every day; if I had been punished for them when I was little they would not be such a trouble to me now."

His ring pricked him very often, and sometimes he left off what he was doing at once; but at other times he would not attend to it. Strangely enough, it gave him only a slight prick for a trifling fault, but when he was really naughty it made his finger actually bleed. At last he got tired of being constantly reminded, and wanted to be able to do as he liked, so he threw his ring aside, and thought himself the happiest of men to have got rid of its teasing pricks. He gave himself up to doing every foolish thing that occurred to him, until he became quite wicked and nobody could like him any longer.

One day, when the Prince was walking about, he saw a young girl who was so very pretty that he made up his mind at once that he would marry her. Her name was Celia, and she was as good as she was beautiful.

Prince Darling fancied that Celia would think herself only too happy if he offered to make her a great queen, but she said fearlessly:

"Sire, I am only a shepherdess, and a poor girl, but, nevertheless, I will not marry you."

"Do you dislike me?" asked the Prince, who was very much vexed at this answer.

"No, my Prince," replied Celia; "I cannot help thinking you very handsome; but what good would riches be to me, and all the grand dresses and splendid carriages that you would give me, if the bad deeds which I should see you do every day made me hate and despise you?"

The Prince was very angry at this speech, and commanded his officers to make Celia a prisoner and carry her off to his palace. All day long the remembrance of what she had said annoyed him, but as he loved her he could not make up his mind to have her punished.

One of the Prince's favorite companions was his foster-brother, whom he trusted entirely; but he was not at all a good man, and gave Prince Darling very bad advice, and encouraged him in all his evil ways. When he saw the Prince so downcast he asked what was the matter, and when he explained that he could not bear Celia's bad opinion of him, and was resolved to be a better man in order to please her, this evil adviser said to him:

"You are very kind to trouble yourself about this little girl; if I were you I would soon make her obey me. Remember that you are a king, and that it would be laughable to see you trying to please a shepherdess, who ought to be only too glad to be one of your slaves. Keep her in prison, and feed her on bread and water for a little while, and then, if she still says she will not marry you, have her kept in hospital, to teach other people that you mean to be obeyed. Why, if you cannot make a girl like that do as you wish, your subjects will soon forget that they are only put into this world for our pleasure."

"But," said Prince Darling, "would it not be a shame if I had an innocent girl put to death? For Celia has done nothing to deserve punishment."

"If people will not do as you tell them they ought to suffer for it," answered his foster-brother; "but even if it were unjust, you had better be accused of that by your subjects than that they should find out that they may insult and thwart you as often as they please."

In saying this he was touching a weak point in his brother's character; for the Prince's fear of losing any of his power made him at once abandon his first idea of trying to be good, and resolve to try and frighten the shepherdess into consenting to marry him.

His foster-brother, who wanted him to keep this resolution, invited three young courtiers, as wicked as himself to sup with the Prince, and they persuaded him to drink a great deal of wine, and continued to excite his anger against Celia by telling him that she had laughed at his love for her; until at last, in quite a furious rage, he rushed off to find her, declaring that if she still refused to marry him she should be sold as a slave the very next day.

But when he reached the room in which Celia had been locked up, he was greatly surprised to find that she was not in it, though he had the key in his own pocket all the time. His anger was terrible, and he vowed vengeance against whoever had helped her to escape. His bad friends, when they heard him, resolved to turn his wrath upon an old nobleman who had formerly been his tutor; and who still dared sometimes to tell the Prince of his faults, for he loved him as if he had been his own son. At first Prince Darling had thanked him, but after a time he grew impatient and thought it must be just mere love of fault-finding that made his old tutor blame him when everyone else was praising and flattering him. So he ordered him to retire from his Court, though he still, from time to time, spoke of him as a worthy man whom he respected, even if he no longer loved him. His unworthy friends feared that he might some day take it into his head to recall his old tutor, so they thought they now had a good opportunity of getting him banished for ever.

They reported to the Prince that Suliman, for that was the tutor's name, had boasted of having helped Celia to escape, and they bribed three men to say that Suliman himself had told them about it. The Prince, in great anger, sent his foster-brother with a number of soldiers to bring his tutor before him, in chains, like a criminal. After giving this order he went to his own room, but he had scarcely got into it when there was a clap of thunder which made the ground shake, and the Fairy Truth appeared suddenly before him.

"I promised your father," said she sternly, "to give you good advice, and to punish you if you refused to follow it. You have despised my counsel, and have gone your own evil way until you are only outwardly a man; really you are a monster—the horror of everyone who knows you. It is time that I should fulfil my promise, and begin your punishment. I condemn you to resemble the animals whose ways you have imitated. You have made yourself like the lion by your anger, and like the wolf by your greediness. Like a snake, you have ungratefully turned upon one who was a second father to you; your churlishness has made you like a bull. Therefore, in your new form, take the appearance of all these animals."

The Fairy had scarcely finished speaking when Prince Darling saw to his horror that her words were fulfilled. He had a lion's head, a bull's horns, a wolf's feet, and a snake's body. At the same instant he found himself in a great forest, beside a clear lake, in which he could see plainly the horrible creature he had become, and a voice said to him:

"Look carefully at the state to which your wickedness has brought you; believe me, your soul is a thousand times more hideous than your body."

Prince Darling recognized the voice of the Fairy Truth and turned in a fury to catch her and eat her up if he possibly could; but he saw no one, and the same voice went on:

"I laugh at your powerlessness and anger, and I intend to punish your pride by letting you fall into the hands of your own subjects."

The Prince began to think that the best thing he could do would be to get as far away from the lake as he could, then at least he would not be continually reminded of his terrible ugliness. So he ran toward the wood, but before he had gone many yards he fell into a deep pit which had been made to trap bears, and the hunters, who were hiding in a tree, leaped down, and secured him with several chains, and led him into the chief city of his own kingdom.

On the way, instead of recognizing that his own faults had brought this punishment upon him, he accused the Fairy of being the cause of all his misfortunes, and bit and tore at his chains furiously.

As they approached the town he saw that some great rejoicing was being held, and when the hunters asked what had happened they were told that the Prince, whose only pleasure it was to torment his people, had been found in his room, killed by a thunder-bolt (for that was what was supposed to have become of him). Four of his courtiers, those who had encouraged him in his wicked doings, had tried to seize the kingdom and divide it between them, but the people, who knew it was their bad counsels which had so changed the Prince, had imprisoned them, and had offered the crown to Suliman, whom the Prince had left in prison. This noble lord had just been crowned, and the deliverance of the kingdom was the cause of the rejoicing "For," they said, "he is a good and just man, and we shall once more enjoy peace and prosperity."

Prince Darling roared with anger when he heard this; but it was still worse for him when he reached the great square before his own palace. He saw Suliman seated upon a magnificent throne, and all the people crowded round, wishing him a long life that he might undo all the mischief done by his predecessor.

Presently Suliman made a sign with his hand that the people should be silent, and said: "I have accepted the crown you have offered me, but only that I may keep it for Prince Darling, who is not dead as you suppose; the Fairy has assured me that there is still hope that you may some day see him again, good and virtuous as he was when he first came to the throne. Alas!" he continued, "he was led away by flatterers. I knew his heart, and am certain that if it had not been for the bad influence of those who surrounded him he would have been a good king and a father to his people. We may hate his faults, but let us pity him and hope for his restoration. As for me, I would die gladly if that could bring back our Prince to reign justly and worthily once more."

These words went to Prince Darling's heart; he realized the true affection and faithfulness of his old tutor, and for the first time reproached himself for all his evil deeds; at the same instant he felt all his anger melting away, and he began quickly to think over his past life, and to admit that his punishment was not more than he had deserved. He left off tearing at the iron bars of the cage in which he was shut up, and became as gentle as a lamb.

The hunters who had caught him took him to a great menagerie, where he was chained up among all the other wild beasts, and he determined to show his sorrow for his past bad behavior by being gentle and obedient to the man who had to take care of him. Unfortunately, this man was very rough and unkind, and though the poor monster was quite quiet, he often beat him without rhyme or reason when he happened to be in a bad temper. One day when this keeper was asleep a tiger broke its chain, and flew at him to eat him up. Prince Darling, who saw what was going on, at first felt quite pleased to think that he should be delivered from his persecutor, but soon thought better of it and wished that he were free.

"I would return good for evil," he said to himself, "and save the unhappy man's life." He had hardly wished this when his iron cage flew open, and he rushed to the side of the keeper, who was awake and was defending himself against the tiger. When he saw the monster had got out he gave himself up for lost, but his fear was soon changed into joy, for the kind monster threw itself upon the tiger and very soon killed it, and then came and crouched at the feet of the man it had saved.

Overcome with gratitude, the keeper stooped to caress the strange creature which had done him such a great service; but suddenly a voice said in his ear:

"A good action should never go unrewarded," and at the same instant the monster disappeared, and he saw at his feet only a pretty little dog!

Prince Darling, delighted by the change, frisked about the keeper, showing his joy in every way he could, and the man, taking him up in his arms, carried him to the King, to whom he told the whole story.

The Queen said she would like to have this wonderful little dog, and the Prince would have been very happy in his new home if he could have forgotten that he was a man and a king. The Queen petted and took care of him, but she was so afraid that he would get too fat that she consulted the court physician, who said that he was to be fed only upon bread, and was not to have much even of that. So poor Prince Darling was terribly hungry all day long, but he was very patient about it.

One day, when they gave him his little loaf for breakfast, he thought he would like to eat it out in the garden; so he took it up in his mouth and trotted away toward a brook that he knew of a long way from the palace. But he was surprised to find that the brook was gone, and where it had been stood a great house that seemed to be built of gold and precious stones. Numbers of people splendidly dressed were going into it, and sounds of music and dancing and feasting could be heard from the windows.

But what seemed very strange was that those people who came out of the house were pale and thin, and their clothes were torn, and hanging in rags about them. Some fell down dead as they came out before they had time to get away; others crawled farther with great difficulty; while others again lay on the ground, fainting with hunger, and begged a morsel of bread from those who were going into the house, but they would not so much as look at the poor creatures.

Prince Darling went up to a young girl who was trying to eat a few blades of grass, she was so hungry. Touched with compassion, he said to himself:

"I am very hungry, but I shall not die of starvation before I get my dinner; if I give my breakfast to this poor creature perhaps I may save her life."

So he laid his piece of bread in the girl's hand, and saw her eat it up eagerly.

She soon seemed to be quite well again, and the Prince, delighted to have been able to help her, was thinking of going home to the palace, when he heard a great outcry, and, turning round, saw Celia, who was being carried against her will into the great house.

For the first time the Prince regretted that he was no longer the monster, then he would have been able to rescue Celia;

now he could only bark feebly at the people who were carrying her off, and try to follow them, but they chased and kicked him away.

He determined not to quit the place till he knew what had become of Celia, and blamed himself for what had befallen her.

"Alas!" he said to himself, "I am furious with the people who are carrying Celia off, but isn't that exactly what I did myself, and if I had not been prevented did I not intend to be still more cruel to her?"

Here he was interrupted by a noise above his head—someone was opening a window, and he saw with delight that it was Celia herself, who came forward and threw out a plate of most delicious-looking food, then the window was shut again, and Prince Darling, who had not had anything to eat all day, thought he might as well take the opportunity of getting something. He ran forward to begin, but the young girl to whom he had given his bread gave a cry of terror and took him up in her arms, saying:

"Don't touch it, my poor little dog—that house is the palace of pleasure, and everything that comes out of it is poisoned!"

At the same moment a voice said:

"You see a good action always brings its reward," and the Prince found himself changed into a beautiful white dove. He remembered that white was the favorite color of the Fairy Truth, and began to hope that he might at last win back her favor. But just now his first care was for Celia, and rising into the air he flew round and round the house, until he saw an open window; but he searched through every room in vain. No trace of Celia was to be seen, and the Prince, in despair, determined to search through the world till he found her. He flew on and on for several days, till he came to a great desert, where he saw a cavern, and, to his delight, there sat Celia, sharing the simple breakfast of an old hermit.

Overjoyed to have found her, Prince Darling perched upon her shoulder, trying to express by his caresses how glad he was to see her again, and Celia, surprised and delighted by the tameness of this pretty white dove, stroked it softly, and said, though she never thought of its understanding her:

"I accept the gift that you make me of yourself, and I will love you always."

"Take care what you are saying, Celia," said the old hermit; "are you prepared to keep that promise?"

"Indeed, I hope so, my sweet shepherdess," cried the Prince, who was at that moment restored to his natural shape. "You promised to love me always; tell me that you really mean what you said, or I shall have to ask the Fairy to give me back the form of the dove which pleased you so much."

"You need not be afraid that she will change her mind," said the Fairy, throwing off the hermit's robe in which she had been disguised and appearing before them.

"Celia has loved you ever since she first saw you, only she would not tell you while you were so obstinate and naughty. Now you have repented and mean to be good you deserve to be happy, and so she may love you as much as she likes."

Celia and Prince Darling threw themselves at the Fairy's feet, and the Prince was never tired of thanking her for her kindness. Celia was delighted to hear how sorry he was for all his past follies and misdeeds, and promised to love him as long as she lived.

"Rise, my children," said the Fairy, "and I will transport you to the palace, and Prince Darling shall have back again the crown he forfeited by his bad behavior."

While she was speaking, they found themselves in Suliman's hall, and his delight was great at seeing his dear master once more. He gave up the throne joyfully to the Prince, and remained always the most faithful of his subjects.

Celia and Prince Darling reigned for many years, but he was so determined to govern worthily and to do his duty that his ring, which he took to wearing again, never once pricked him severely.

Rose of evening

On the fifth day of the fifth month the festival of the Dragon Junk is held along the Yangtze-kiang. A dragon is hollowed out of wood, painted with an armor of scales, and adorned with gold and bright colors. A carved red railing surrounds this ship, and its sails and flags are made of silks and brocade. The after part of the vessel is called the dragon's tail. It rises ten feet above the water, and a board which floats in the water is tied to it by means of a cloth. Upon this board sit boys who turn somersaults, stand on their heads, and perform all sorts of tricks. Yet, being so close to the water their danger is very great. It is the custom, therefore, when a boy is hired for this purpose, to give his parents money before he is trained. Then, if he falls into the water and is drowned, no one has him on their conscience. Farther South the custom differs in so much that instead of boys, beautiful girls are chosen for this purpose.

In Dschen-Giang there once lived a widow named Dsiang, who had a son called Aduan. When he was no more than seven years of age he was extraordinarily skilful, and no other boy could equal him. And his reputation increasing as he grew, he earned more and more money. So it happened that he was still called upon at the Dragon Junk Festival when he was already sixteen.

But one day he fell into the water below the Gold Island and was drowned. He was the only son of his mother, and she sorrowed over him, and that was the end of it.

Yet Aduan did not know that he had been drowned. He met two men who took him along with them, and he saw a new world in the midst of the waters of the Yellow River. When he looked around, the waves of the river towered steeply about him like walls, and a palace was visible, in which sat a man wearing armor and a helmet. His two companions said to him: "That is the Prince of the Dragon's Cave!" and bade him kneel.

The Prince of the Dragon's Cave seemed to be of a mild and kindly disposition and said: "We can make use of such a skilful lad. He may take part in the dance of the willow branches!"

So he was brought to a spot surrounded by extensive buildings. He entered, and was greeted by a crowd of boys who were all about fourteen years of age.

An old woman came in and they all called out: "This is Mother Hia!" And she sat down and had Aduan show his tricks. Then she taught him the dance of the flying thunders of Tsian-Tang River, and the music that calms the winds on the sea of Dung-Ting. When the cymbals and kettledrums reechoed through all the courts, they deafened the ear. Then, again, all the courts would fall silent. Mother Hia thought that Aduan would not be able to grasp everything the very first time; so she taught him with great patience. But Aduan had understood everything from the first, and that pleased old Mother Hia. "This boy," said she, "equals our own Rose of Evening!"

The following day the Prince of the Dragon's Cave held a review of his dancers. When all the dancers had assembled, the dance of the Ogres was danced first. Those who performed it all wore devil-masks and garments of scales. They beat upon enormous cymbals, and their kettledrums were so large that four men could just about span them. Their sound was like the sound of a mighty thunder, and the noise was so great that nothing else could be heard. When the dance began, tremendous waves spouted up to the very skies, and then fell down again like star-glimmer which scatters in the air.

The Prince of the Dragon Cave hastily bade the dance cease, and had the dancers of the nightingale round step forth. These were all lovely young girls of sixteen. They made a delicate music with flutes, so that the breeze blew and the roaring of the waves was stilled in a moment. The water gradually became as quiet as a crystal world, transparent to its lowest depths. When the nightingale dancers had finished, they withdrew and posted themselves in the western courtyard.

Then came the turn of the swallow dancers. These were all little girls. One among them, who was about fifteen years of age, danced the dance of the giving of flowers with flying sleeves and waving locks. And as their garments fluttered, many-colored flowers dropped from their folds, and were caught up by the wind and whirled about the whole courtyard. When the dance had ended, this dancer also went off with the rest of the girls to the western courtyard. Aduan looked at her from out the corner of his eye, and fell deeply in love with her. He asked his comrades who she might be and they told him she was named "Rose of Evening."

But the willow-spray dancers were now called out. The Prince of the Dragon Cave was especially desirous of testing Aduan. So Aduan danced alone, and he danced with joy or defiance according to the music. When he looked up and when he looked down his glances held the beat of the measure. The

Dragon Prince, enchanted with his skill, presented him with a garment of five colors, and gave him a carbuncle set in golden threads of fish-beard for a hair-jewel. Aduan bowed his thanks for the gift, and then also hastened to the western courtyard. There all the dancers stood in rank and file. Aduan could only look at Rose of Evening from a distance, but still Rose of Evening returned his glances.

After a time Aduan gradually slipped to the end of his file and Rose of Evening also drew near to him, so that they stood only a few feet away from each other. But the strict rules allowed no confusion in the ranks, so they could only gaze and let their souls go out to each other.

Now the butterfly dance followed the others. This was danced by the boys and girls together, and the pairs were equal in size, age and the color of their garments. When all the dances had ended, the dancers marched out with the goose-step. The willow-spray dancers followed the swallow dancers, and Aduan hastened in advance of his company, while Rose of Evening lingered along after hers. She turned her head, and when she spied Aduan she purposely let a coral pin fall from her hair. Aduan hastily hid it in his sleeve.

When he had returned, he was sick with longing, and could neither eat nor sleep. Mother Hia brought him all sorts of dainties, looked after him three or four times a day, and stroked his forehead with loving care. But his illness did not yield in the least. Mother Hia was unhappy, and yet helpless.

"The birthday of the King of the Wu River is at hand," said she. "What is to be done?"

In the twilight there came a boy, who sat down on the edge of Aduan's bed and chatted with him. He belonged to the butterfly dancers, said he, and asked casually: "Are you sick because of Rose of Evening?" Aduan, frightened, asked him how he came to guess it. The other boy said, with a smile: "Well, because Rose of Evening is in the same case as yourself."

Disconcerted, Aduan sat up and begged the boy to advise him. "Are you able to walk?" asked the latter. "If I exert myself," said Aduan, "I think I could manage it."

So the boy led him to the South. There he opened a gate and they turned the corner, to the West. Once more the doors of the gate flew open, and now Aduan saw a lotus field about twenty acres in size. The lotus flowers were all growing on level earth, and their leaves were as large as mats and their flowers like umbrellas. The fallen blossoms covered the ground beneath the stalks to the depth of a foot or more. The boy led Aduan in and said, "Now first of all sit down for a little while!" Then he went away.

After a time a beautiful girl thrust aside the lotus flowers and came into the open. It was Rose of Evening. They looked at each other with happy timidity, and each told how each had longed for the other. And they also told each other of their former life. Then they weighted the lotus-leaves with stones so that they made a cozy retreat, in which they could be together, and promised to meet each other there every evening. And then they parted.

Aduan came back and his illness left him. From that time on he met Rose of Evening every day in the lotus field.

After a few days had passed they had to accompany the Prince of the Dragon Cave to the birthday festival of the King of the Wu River. The festival came to an end, and all the dancers returned home. Only, the King had kept back Rose of Evening and one of the nightingale dancers to teach the girls in his castle.

Months passed and no news came from Rose of Evening, so that Aduan went about full of longing and despair. Now Mother Hia went every day to the castle of the god of the Wu River. So Aduan told her that Rose of Evening was his cousin, and entreated her to take him along with her so that he could at least see her a single time. So she took him along, and let him stay at the lodge-house of the river-god for a few days. But the indwellers of the castle were so strictly watched that he could not see Rose of Evening even a single time. Sadly Aduan went back again.

Another month passed and Aduan, filled with gloomy thoughts, wished that death might be his portion.

One day Mother Hia came to him full of pity, and began to sympathize with him. "What a shame," said she, "that Rose of Evening has cast herself into the river!"

Aduan was extremely frightened, and his tears flowed resistlessly. He tore his beautiful garments, took his gold and his pearls, and went out with the sole idea of following his beloved in death. Yet the waters of the river stood up before him like walls, and no matter how often he ran against them, head down, they always flung him back.

He did not dare return, since he feared he might be questioned about his festival garments, and severely punished because he had ruined them. So he stood there and knew not what to do, while the perspiration ran down to his ankles. Suddenly, at the foot of the water-wall he saw a tall tree. Like a monkey he climbed up to its very top, and then, with all his might, he shot into the waves.

And then, without being wet, he found himself suddenly swimming on the surface of the river. Unexpectedly the world of men rose up once more before his dazzled eyes. He swam to the shore, and as he walked along the river-bank, his thoughts went back to his old mother. He took a ship and traveled home.

When he reached the village, it seemed to him as though all the houses in it belonged to another world. The following morning he entered his mother's house, and as he did so, heard a girl's voice beneath the window saying: "Your son has come back again!" The voice sounded like the voice of Rose of Evening, and when she came to greet him at his mother's side, sure enough, it was Rose of Evening herself.

And in that hour the joy of these two who were so fond of each other overcame all their sorrow. But in the mother's mind sorrow and doubt, terror and joy mingled in constant succession in a thousand different ways.

When Rose of Evening had been in the palace of the river-king, and had come to realize that she would never see Aduan again, she determined to die, and flung herself into the waters of the stream. But she was carried to the surface, and the waves carried and cradled her till a ship came by and took her aboard. They asked whence she came. Now Rose of Evening had originally been a celebrated singing girl of Wu, who had fallen into the river and whose body had never been found. So she thought to herself that, after all, she could not return to her old life again. So she answered: "Madame Dsiang, in Dschen-Giang is my mother-in-law." Then the travelers took passage for her in a ship which brought her to the place she had mentioned. The widow Dsiang first said she must be mistaken, but the girl insisted that there was no mistake, and told Aduan's mother her whole story. Yet, though the latter was charmed by her surpassing loveliness, she feared that Rose of Evening was too young to live a widow's life. But the girl was respectful and industrious, and when she saw that poverty ruled in her new home, she took her pearls and sold them for a high price. Aduan's old mother was greatly pleased to see how seriously the girl took her duties.

Now that Aduan had returned again Rose of Evening could not control her joy. And even Aduan's old mother cherished the hope that, after all, perhaps her son had not died. She secretly dug up her son's grave, yet all his bones were still lying in it. So she questioned Aduan. And then, for the first time, the latter realized that he was a departed spirit. Then he feared that Rose of Evening might regard him with disgust because he was no longer a human being. So he ordered his mother on no account to speak of it, and this his mother promised. Then she spread the report in the village that the body which had been found in the river had not been that of her son at all. Yet she could not rid herself of the fear that, since Aduan was a departed spirit, heaven might refuse to send him a child.

In spite of her fear, however, she was able to hold a grandson in her arms in course of time. When she looked at him, he was no different from other children, and then her cup of joy was filled to overflowing.

Rose of Evening gradually became aware of the fact that Aduan was not really a human being. "Why did you not tell me at once?" said she. "Departed spirits who wear the garments of the dragon castle, surround themselves with a soul-casing so heavy in texture that they can no longer be distinguished from the living. And if one can obtain the lime made of dragon-horn which is in the castle, then the bones may be glued together in such wise that flesh and blood will grow over them again. What a pity that we could not obtain the lime while we were there!"

Aduan sold his pearl, for which a merchant from foreign parts gave him an enormous sum. Thus his family grew very wealthy. Once, on his mother's birthday, he danced with his wife and sang, in order to please her. The news reached the castle of the Dragon Prince and he thought to carry off Rose of Evening by force. But Aduan, alarmed, went to the Prince, and declared that both he and his wife were departed spirits. They examined him and since he cast no shadow, his word was taken, and he was not robbed of Rose of Evening.

The cat who could eat so much

ONCE upon a time there was a man who had a cat, and she ate so very much that he did not want to keep her any longer. So he decided to give her away; but before he did so she was to have something to eat just once more. The woman offered her a dish of mush and a little potful of fat. These she swallowed, and then jumped out of the window. There stood the man on the threshing-floor.

"Good-day, man in the house," said the cat.

"Good-day, cat," said the man. "Have you had anything to eat yet to-day?"

"O, only a little, but my fast has hardly been broken," said the cat. "I have had no more than a dish of mush and a little potful of fat, and I am thinking over whether I ought not to eat you as well," said she, and she seized the man and ate him up. Then she went into the stable. There sat the woman, milking.

"Good-day, woman in the stable," said the cat.

"Good-day, cat, is that you?" said the woman. "Have you eaten your food?" she asked.

"O, only a little to-day. My fast has hardly been broken," said the cat. "I have had no more than a dish of mush and a little potful of fat and the man in the house, and I'm thinking over whether I ought not to eat you as well," said she, and she seized the woman and ate her up.

"Good-day, cow at the manger," said the cat to the bell-cow.

"Good-day, cat," said the bell-cow. "Have you had anything to eat yet to-day?" "O, only a little. My fast has hardly been broken," said the cat. "I have had no more than a dish of mush and a little potful of fat and the man in the house and the woman in the stable, and I'm thinking over whether I ought not to eat you as well," said the cat, and seized the bell-cow and ate her up. Then she went up to the orchard, and there stood a man who was sweeping up leaves.

"Good-day, leaf-sweeper in the orchard," said the cat.

"Good-day, cat," said the man. "Have you had anything to eat yet to-day?"

"O, only a little. My fast has hardly been broken," said the cat. "I have had no more than a dish of mush and a little potful of fat and the man in the house and the woman in the stable and the bell-cow at the manger, and I'm thinking over whether I ought not to eat you up as well," said she, and seized the leaf-sweeper and ate him up.

Then she came to a stone-pile. There stood the weasel, looking about him.

"Good-day, weasel on the stone-pile," said the cat.

"Good-day, cat," said the weasel. "Have you had anything to eat yet to-day?"

"O, only a little. My fast has hardly been broken," said the cat. "I have had no more than a dish of mush and a little potful of fat and the man in the house and the woman in the stable and the bell-cow at the manger and the leaf-sweeper in the orchard, and I'm thinking over whether I ought not to eat you as well," said the cat, and seized the weasel and ate him up.

After she had gone a while, she came to a hazel-bush. There sat the squirrel, gathering nuts.

"Good-day, squirrel in the bush," said the cat.

"Good-day, cat! Have you already had anything to eat yet to-day?" said the squirrel.

"O, only a little. My fast has hardly been broken," said the cat. "I have had no more than a dish of mush and a little potful of fat and the man in the house and the woman in the stable and the bell-cow at the manger and the leaf-sweeper in the orchard and the weasel on the stone-pile, and I'm thinking over whether I ought not to eat you up as well," said she, and seized the squirrel and ate him up.

After she had gone a little while longer, she met Reynard the fox, who was peeping out of the edge of the forest.

"Good-day, fox, you sly-boots," said the cat.

"Good-day, cat! Have you had anything to eat yet to-day?" said the fox.

"O, only a little. My fast has hardly been broken," said the cat. "I have had no more than a dish of mush and a little potful of fat and the man in the house and the woman in the stable and the bell-cow at the manger and the leaf-sweeper in the orchard and the weasel on the stone-pile and the squirrel in the hazel-bush, and I'm thinking over whether I ought not to eat you as well," said she, and seized the fox and ate him up too.

When she had gone a little further, she met a hare.

"Good-day, you hopping hare," said the cat.

"Good-day, cat! Have you had anything to eat yet to-day?" said the hare.

"O, only a little. My fast has hardly been broken," said the cat. "I have had no more than a dish of mush and a little potful of fat and the man in the house and the woman in the stable and the bell-cow at the manger and the leaf-sweeper in the orchard and the weasel on the stone-pile and the squirrel in the hazel-bush and the fox, the sly-boots, and I'm thinking over whether I ought not to eat you up as well," said she, and seized the hare and ate him up.

When she had gone a little further, she met a wolf.

"Good-day, you wild wolf," said the cat.

"Good-day, cat! Have you had anything to eat yet to-day?" said the wolf.

"O, only a little. My fast has hardly been broken," said the cat. "I have had no more than a dish of mush and a little potful of fat and the man in the house and the woman in the stable and the bell-cow at the manger and the leaf-sweeper in the orchard and the weasel on the stone-pile and the squirrel in the hazel-bush and the fox, the sly-boots, and the hopping hare, and I'm thinking over whether I ought not to eat you up as well," said she, and seized the wolf and ate him up, too.

Then she went into the wood, and when she had gone far and farther than far, over hill and dale, she met a young bear.

"Good-day, little bear brown-coat," said the cat.

"Good-day, cat! Have you had anything to eat yet to-day?" said the bear.

"O, only a little. My fast has hardly been broken," said the cat. "I have had no more than a dish of mush and a little pot of fat and the man in the house and the woman in the stable and the bell-cow at the manger and the leaf-sweeper in the orchard and the weasel on the stone-pile and the squirrel in the hazel-bush and the fox, the sly-boots, and the hopping hare and the wild wolf, and I'm thinking over whether I ought not to eat you up as well," said she, and seized the little bear and ate him up.

When the cat had gone a bit further, she met the mother bear, who was clawing at the tree-stems so that the bark flew, so angry was she to have lost her little one.

"Good-day, you biting mother bear," said the cat.

"Good-day, cat! Have you had anything to eat yet to-day?" said the mother bear.

"O, only a little. My fast has hardly been broken," said the cat. "I have had no more than a dish of mush and a little potful of fat and the man in the house and the woman in the stable and the bell-cow[160] at the manger and the leaf-sweeper in the orchard and the weasel on the stone-pile and the squirrel in the hazel-bush and the fox, the sly-boots, and the hopping hare and the wild wolf and the little bear brown-coat, and I'm thinking over whether I ought not to eat you as well," said she, and seized the mother bear and ate her, too.

When the cat had gone on a little further, she met the bear himself.

"Good-day, Bruin Good-fellow," said she.

"Good-day, cat! Have you had anything to eat yet to-day?" asked the bear.

"O, only a little. My fast has hardly been broken," said the cat. "I have had no more than a dish of mush and a little potful of fat and the man in the house and the woman in the stable and the bell-cow at the manger and the leaf-sweeper in the orchard and the weasel in the stone-pile and the squirrel in the hazel-bush and the fox, the sly-boots, and the hopping hare and the wild wolf and the little bear brown-coat and the biting mother bear, and now I'm thinking over whether I ought not to eat you as well," said she, and she seized the bear and ate him up, too.

Then the cat went far and farther than far, until she came into the parish. And there she met a bridal party on the road.

"Good-day, bridal party on the road," said the cat.

"Good-day, cat! Have you had anything to eat yet to-day?"

"O, only a little. My fast is hardly broken," said the cat. "I have had no more than a dish of mush and a little potful of fat and the man in the house and the woman in the stable and the bell-cow at the manger and the leaf-sweeper in the orchard and the weasel on the stone-pile and the squirrel in the hazel-bush and the fox, the sly-boots, and the hopping hare and the wild wolf and the little bear brown-coat and the biting mother bear and bruin good-fellow and now I'm thinking whether I ought not to eat you up as well," said she, and she pounced on the whole bridal party, and ate it up, with the cook, the musicians, the horses and all.

When she had gone a bit farther, she came to the church. And there she met a funeral procession.

"Good-day, funeral procession at the church," said the cat.

"Good-day, cat! Have you had anything to eat yet to-day?" said the funeral procession.

"O, only a little. My fast has hardly been broken," said the cat. "I have had no more than a dish of mush and a little potful of fat and the man in the house and the woman in the stable and the bell-cow at the manger and the leaf-sweeper in the orchard and the weasel on the stone-pile and the squirrel in the hazel-bush and the fox, the sly-boots, and the hopping hare and the wild wolf and little bear brown-coat and the biting mother bear and bruin good-fellow and the bridal party on the road, and now I'm thinking over whether I ought not to eat you up as well," said she, and pounced on the funeral procession, and ate up corpse and procession.

When the cat had swallowed it all, she went straight on up to the sky, and when she had gone far and farther than far, she met the moon in a cloud.

"Good-day, moon in a cloud," said the cat.

"Good-day, cat! Have you had anything to eat yet to-day?" said the moon.

"O, only a little. My fast has hardly been broken," said the cat. "I have had no more than a dish of mush and a little potful of fat and the man in the house and the woman in the stable and the bell-cow at the manger and the leaf-sweeper in the orchard and the weasel on the stone-pile and the squirrel in the hazel-bush and the fox, the sly-boots, and the wild wolf and little bear brown-coat and the biting mother bear and bruin good-fellow and the bridal party on the road and the funeral procession at the church, and now I'm thinking over whether I ought not to eat you up as well," said she, and pounced on the moon and ate him up, half and full.

Then the cat went far and farther than far, and met the sun.

"Good morning, cat! Have you had anything to eat yet to-day?" said the sun.

"O, only a little," said the cat. "I have had no more than a dish of mush and a little potful of fat and the man in the house and the woman in the stable and the bell-cow at the manger and the leaf-sweeper in the orchard and the weasel on the stone-pile and the squirrel in the hazel-bush and the fox, the sly-boots, and the hopping hare and the wild wolf and little bear brown-coat and the biting mother bear and bruin good-fellow and the bridal party on the road and the funeral procession at the church and the moon in a cloud, and now I'm thinking over whether I ought not to eat you up as well," said she, and pounced on the sun in the sky and ate him up.

Then the cat went far and farther than far, until she came to a bridge, and there she met a large billy-goat.
"Good morning, billy-goat on the broad bridge," said the cat.
"Good morning, cat! Have you had anything to eat yet to-day?" said the goat.
"O, only a little. My fast has hardly been broken," said the cat. "I had no more than a dish of mush and a little potful of fat and the man in the house and the woman in the stable and the bell-cow at the manger and the leaf-sweeper in the orchard and the weasel on the stone-pile and the squirrel in the hazel-bush and the fox, the sly-boots, and the hopping hare and the wild wolf and little bear brown-coat and the biting mother bear and bruin good-fellow and the bridal party on the road and the funeral procession at the church and the moon in a cloud and the sun in the sky, and now I'm thinking over whether I ought not to eat you up as well," said she.
"We'll fight about that first of all," said the goat, and butted the cat with his horns so that she rolled off the bridge, and fell into the water, and there she burst.
Then they all crawled out, and each went to his own place, all whom the cat had eaten up, and were every one of them as lively as before, the man in the house and the woman in the stable and the bell-cow at the manger and the leaf-sweeper in the orchard and the weasel on the stone-pile and the squirrel in the hazel-bush and the fox, the sly-boots, and the hopping hare and the wild wolf and little bear brown-coat and the biting mother bear and bruin good-fellow and the bridal party

on the road and the funeral procession at the church and the moon in a cloud and the sun in the sky.

Princess Hase

Many, many years ago there lived in Nara, the ancient Capital of Japan, a wise State minister, by name Prince Toyonari Fujiwara. His wife was a noble, good, and beautiful woman called Princess Murasaki (Violet). They had been married by their respective families according to Japanese custom when very young, and had lived together happily ever since. They had, however, one cause for great sorrow, for as the years went by no child was born to them. This made them very unhappy, for they both longed to see a child of their own who would grow up to gladden their old age, carry on the family name, and keep up the ancestral rites when they were dead.

The Prince and his lovely wife, after long consultation and much thought, determined to make a pilgrimage to the temple of Hase-no-Kwannon (Goddess of Mercy at Hase), for they believed, according to the beautiful tradition of their religion, that the Mother of Mercy, Kwannon, comes to answer the prayers of mortals in the form that they need the most. Surely after all these years of prayer she would come to them in the form of a beloved child in answer to their special pilgrimage, for that was the greatest need of their two lives. Everything else they had that this life could give them, but it was all as nothing because the cry of their hearts was unsatisfied.

So the Prince Toyonari and his wife went to the temple of Kwannon at Hase and stayed there for a long time, both daily offering incense and praying to Kwannon, the Heavenly Mother, to grant them the desire of their whole lives. And their prayer was answered.

A daughter was born at last to the Princess Murasaki, and great was the joy of her heart. On presenting the child to her husband, they both decided to call her Hase-Hime, or the Princess of Hase, because she was the gift of the Kwannon at that place. They both reared her with great care and tenderness, and the child grew in strength and beauty.

When the little girl was five years old her mother fell dangerously ill and all the doctors and their medicines could not save her. A little before she breathed her last she called her daughter to her, and gently stroking her head, said:

"Hase-Hime, do you know that your mother cannot live any longer? Though I die, you must grow up a good girl. Do your best not to give trouble to your nurse or any other of your family. Perhaps your father will marry again and some one will fill my place as your mother. If so do not grieve for me, but look upon your father's second wife as your true mother, and be obedient and filial to both her and your father. Remember when you are grown up to be submissive to those who are your superiors, and to be kind to all those who are under you. Don't forget this. I die with the hope that you will grow up a model woman."

Hase-Hime listened in an attitude of respect while her mother spoke, and promised to do all that she was told. There is a proverb which says "As the soul is at three so it is at one hundred," and so Hase-Hime grew up as her mother had wished, a good and obedient little Princess, though she was now too young to understand how great was the loss of her mother.

Not long after the death of his first wife, Prince Toyonari married again, a lady of noble birth named Princess Terute. Very different in character, alas! to the good and wise Princess Murasaki, this woman had a cruel, bad heart. She did not love her step-daughter at all, and was often very unkind to the little motherless girl, saving to herself:

"This is not my child! this is not my child!"

But Hase-Hime bore every unkindness with patience, and even waited upon her step-mother kindly and obeyed her in every way and never gave any trouble, just as she had been trained by her own good mother, so that the Lady Terute had no cause for complaint against her.

The little Princess was very diligent, and her favorite studies were music and poetry. She would spend several hours practicing every day, and her father had the most proficient of masters he could find to teach her the koto (Japanese harp), the art of writing letters and verse. When she was twelve years of age she could play so beautifully that she and her step-mother were summoned to the Palace to perform before the Emperor.

It was the Festival of the Cherry Flowers, and there were great festivities at the Court. The Emperor threw himself into the enjoyment of the season, and commanded that Princess Hase should perform before him on the koto, and that her mother Princess Terute should accompany her on the flute.

The Emperor sat on a raised dais, before which was hung a curtain of finely-sliced bamboo and purple tassels, so that His Majesty might see all and not be seen, for no ordinary subject was allowed to look upon his sacred face.

Hase-Hime was a skilled musician though so young, and often astonished her masters by her wonderful memory and talent. On this momentous occasion she played well. But Princess Terute, her step-mother, who was a lazy woman and never took the trouble to practice daily, broke down in her accompaniment and had to request one of the Court ladies to take her place. This was a great disgrace, and she was furiously jealous to think that she had failed where her step-daughter succeeded; and to make matters worse the Emperor sent many beautiful gifts to the little Princess to reward her for playing so well at the Palace.

There was also now another reason why Princess Terute hated her step-daughter, for she had had the good fortune to have a son born to her, and in her inmost heart she kept saying:

"If only Hase-Hime were not here, my son would have all the love of his father."

And never having learned to control herself, she allowed this wicked thought to grow into the awful desire of taking her step-daughter's life.

So one day she secretly ordered some poison and poisoned some sweet wine. This poisoned wine she put into a bottle. Into another similar bottle she poured some good wine. It was the occasion of the Boys' Festival on the fifth of May, and Hase-Hime was playing with her little brother. All his toys of warriors and heroes were spread out and she was telling him wonderful stories about each of them. They were both enjoying themselves and laughing merrily with their attendants when his mother entered with the two bottles of wine and some delicious cakes.

"You are both so good and happy." said the wicked Princess Terute with a smile, "that I have brought you some sweet wine as a reward—and here are some nice cakes for my good children."

And she filled two cups from the different bottles.

Hase-Hime, never dreaming of the dreadful part her step-mother was acting, took one of the cups of wine and gave to her little step brother the other that had been poured out for him.

The wicked woman had carefully marked the poisoned bottle, but on coming into the room she had grown nervous, and pouring out the wine hurriedly had unconsciously given the poisoned cup to her own child. All this time she was anxiously watching the little Princess, but to her amazement no change whatever took place in the young girl's face. Suddenly the little boy screamed and threw himself on the floor, doubled up with pain. His mother flew to him, taking the precaution to upset the two tiny jars of wine which she had brought into the room, and lifted him up. The attendants rushed for the doctor, but nothing could save the child—he died within the hour in his mother's arms. Doctors did not know much in those ancient times, and it was thought that the wine had disagreed with the boy, causing convulsions of which he died. Thus was the wicked woman punished in losing her own child when she had tried to do away with her step-daughter; but instead of blaming herself she began to hate Hase-Hime more than ever in the bitterness and wretchedness of her own heart, and she eagerly watched for an opportunity to do her harm, which was, however, long in coming.

When Hase-Hime was thirteen years of age, she had already become mentioned as a poetess of some merit. This was an accomplishment very much cultivated by the women of old Japan and one held in high esteem.

It was the rainy season at Nara, and floods were reported every day as doing damage in the neighborhood. The river Tatsuta, which flowed through the Imperial Palace grounds, was swollen to the top of its banks, and the roaring of the torrents of water rushing along a narrow bed so disturbed the Emperor's rest day and night, that a serious nervous disorder was the result. An Imperial Edict was sent forth to all the Buddhist temples commanding the priests to offer up continuous prayers to Heaven to stop the noise of the flood. But this was of no avail.

Then it was whispered in Court circles that the Princess Hase, the daughter of Prince Toyonari Fujiwara, second minister at Court, was the most gifted poetess of the day, though still so young, and her masters confirmed the report. Long ago, a beautiful and gifted maiden-poetess had moved Heaven by praying in verse, had brought down rain upon a land famished with drought—so said the ancient biographers of the poetess Ono-no-Komachi. If the Princess Hase were to write a poem and offer it in prayer, might it not stop the noise of the rushing river and remove the cause of the Imperial illness? What the Court said at last reached the ears of the Emperor himself, and he sent an order to the minister Prince Toyonari to this effect.

Great indeed was Hase-Hime's fear and astonishment when her father sent for her and told her what was required of her. Heavy, indeed, was the duty that was laid on her young shoulders—that of saving the Emperor's life by the merit of her verse.

At last the day came and her poem was finished. It was written on a leaflet of paper heavily flecked with gold-dust. With her father and attendants and some of the Court officials, she proceeded to the bank of the roaring torrent and raising up her heart to Heaven, she read the poem she had composed, aloud, lifting it heavenwards in her two hands.

Strange indeed it seemed to all those standing round. The waters ceased their roaring, and the river was quiet in direct answer to her prayer. After this the Emperor soon recovered his health.

His Majesty was highly pleased, and sent for her to the Palace and rewarded her with the rank of Chinjo—that of Lieutenant-General—to distinguish her. From that time she was called Chinjo-hime, or the Lieutenant-General Princess, and respected and loved by all.

There was only one person who was not pleased at Hase-Hime's success. That one was her stepmother. Forever brooding over the death of her own child whom she had killed when trying to poison her step-daughter, she had the mortification of seeing her rise to power and honor, marked by Imperial favor and the admiration of the whole Court. Her envy and jealousy burned in her heart like fire. Many were the lies she carried to her husband about Hase-Hime, but all to no purpose. He would listen to none of her tales, telling her sharply that she was quite mistaken.

At last the step-mother, seizing the opportunity of her husband's absence, ordered one of her old servants to take the innocent girl to the Hibari Mountains, the wildest part of the country, and to kill her there. She invented a dreadful story about the little Princess, saying that this was the only way to prevent disgrace falling upon the family—by killing her.

Katoda, her vassal, was bound to obey his mistress. Anyhow, he saw that it would be the wisest plan to pretend obedience in the absence of the girl's father, so he placed Hase-Hime in a palanquin and accompanied her to the most solitary place he could find in the wild district. The poor child knew there was no good in protesting to her unkind step-mother at being sent away in this strange manner, so she went as she was told. But the old servant knew that the young Princess was quite innocent of all the things her step-mother had invented to him as reasons for her outrageous orders, and he determined to save her life. Unless he killed her, however, he could not return to his cruel task-mistress, so he decided to stay out in the wilderness. With the help of some peasants he soon built a little cottage, and having sent secretly for his wife to come, these two good old people did all in their power to take care of the now unfortunate Princess. She all the time trusted in her father, knowing that as soon as he returned home and found her absent, he would search for her.

Prince Toyonari, after some weeks, came home, and was told by his wife that his daughter Hime had done something wrong and had run away for fear of being punished. He was nearly ill with anxiety. Every one in the house told the same story—that Hase-Hime had suddenly disappeared, none of them knew why or whither. For fear of scandal he kept the matter quiet and searched everywhere he could think of, but all to no purpose.

One day, trying to forget his terrible worry, he called all his men together and told them to make ready for a several days' hunt in the mountains. They were soon ready and mounted, waiting at the gate for their lord. He rode hard and fast to the district of the Hibari Mountains, a great company following him. He was soon far ahead of every one, and at last found himself in a narrow picturesque valley.

Looking round and admiring the scenery, he noticed a tiny house on one of the hills quite near, and then he distinctly heard a beautiful clear voice reading aloud. Seized with curiosity as to who could be studying so diligently in such a lonely spot, he dismounted, and leaving his horse to his groom, he walked up the hillside and approached the cottage. As he drew nearer his surprise increased, for he could see that the reader was a beautiful girl. The cottage was wide open and she was sitting facing the view. Listening attentively, he heard her reading the Buddhist scriptures with great devotion. More and more curious, he hurried on to the tiny gate and entered the little garden, and looking up beheld his lost daughter Hase-Hime. She was so intent on what she was saying that she neither heard nor saw her father till he spoke.

"Hase-Hime!" he cried, "it is you, my Hase-Hime!"

Taken by surprise, she could hardly realize that it was her own dear father who was calling her, and for a moment she was utterly bereft of the power to speak or move.

"My father, my father! It is indeed you—oh, my father!" was all she could say, and running to him she caught hold of his thick sleeve, and burying her face burst into a passion of tears. Her father stroked her dark hair, asking her gently to tell him all that had happened, but she only wept on, and he wondered if he were not really dreaming.

Then the faithful old servant Katoda came out, and bowing himself to the ground before his master, poured out the long tale of wrong, telling him all that had happened, and how it was that he found his daughter in such a wild and desolate spot with only two old servants to take care of her.

The Prince's astonishment and indignation knew no bounds. He gave up the hunt at once and hurried home with his daughter. One of the company galloped ahead to inform the household of the glad news, and the step-mother hearing what had happened, and fearful of meeting her husband now that her wickedness was discovered, fled from the house and returned in disgrace to her father's roof, and nothing more was heard of her.

The old servant Katoda was rewarded with the highest promotion in his master's service, and lived happily to the end of his days, devoted to the little Princess, who never forgot that she owed her life to this faithful retainer. She was no longer troubled by an unkind step-mother, and her days passed happily and quietly with her father.

As Prince Toyonari had no son, he adopted a younger son of one of the Court nobles to be his heir, and to marry his daughter Hase-Hime, and in a few years the marriage took place. Hase-Hime lived to a good old age, and all said that she was the wisest, most devout, and most beautiful mistress that had ever reigned in Prince Toyonari's ancient house. She had the joy of presenting her son, the future lord of the family, to her father just before he retired from active life.

To this day there is preserved a piece of needle-work in one of the Buddhist temples of Kioto. It is a beautiful piece of tapestry, with the figure of Buddha embroidered in the silky threads drawn from the stem of the lotus. This is said to have been the work of the hands of the good Princess Hase.

4. the floating nights

The night is rising up,
The sun is falling down.
Our fears are going up,
Our hands holding our clothes.
How can we be that star who shines?
When we ourselves aren't even a star
Is there someway to get out of this box?
Because life keeps on flashing on
Everyday, everynight
We dream of something that isn't right
That's why we're afraid of nights
Because we wouldn't know
what's the other fright.

It felt dark, but not uncomfortably so. Sometimes they dimmed the lights or pulled the curtains, but this felt different. He wasn't sure about the darkness – it seemed much darker than normal, but maybe it was night-time; if so, perhaps he should try and sleep.

When he woke again or thought he woke, it was still dark. It could be he was dreaming – he knew he used to dream. He liked those times when he dreamt, he felt free, and he seemed to be able to do what he wanted. But this didn't feel like a dream. Those felt slightly detached, as though he was observing himself and not always really part of the dream.

He liked dreams – he felt strong, and it was usually warm and light in his dreams. He often met other people there, sometimes they would talk to him, but he didn't always seem to be able to talk to them. It never really mattered as the dreams continued whether he spoke or not. The dreams were good, especially the ones where he was outside in the warm sunshine. Perhaps if he slept, he would dream again. He would like to feel the warmth of the sun and the light.

The darkness felt good now – it wasn't cold dark, but then it didn't feel particularly warm either, but it was comforting.

He woke; it was still dark, but he could sense something. His clothes felt different, but then they often did after he woke up. He knew they changed his clothes when he was asleep and probably because he complained if they moved him when he was awake. He didn't like it when they moved him. It was usually just as he was beginning to feel warm and soft and comfortable. The clothes they put on him were always cold and far too hard, but this felt different. The cloth felt soft, but the clothes felt different, somehow not quite lived in but better. Perhaps they had finally listened to him and had got some of his own clothes from home.

Home – he knew he had a home; it was where he lived, but he couldn't remember where it was. They had asked him where he lived, and he told them it was warm and comfortable and there were trees. He liked the trees in the wood; it was his place. He had planted most of the trees himself and had watched them grow from small and delicate saplings to the beautiful, strong trees in the woods. He felt comfortable in the woods. It was quiet in a noisy sort of way.

< 2 >

The trees constantly moved – the wind moved the trees, and the trees responded to the sunlight, but if you listened on a quiet, gentle day, the trees were still moving even at night.

He tried to move his arms and his hands, but they didn't seem to work – maybe he was tired and should try sleeping again. Then, he felt something brush gently against his leg – at least it felt like his leg or where it should be, but he wasn't sure. It was a soft touch, almost a caress. The sort of feeling he remembered from a long time ago. A gently soothing stroke that felt good and brought back pleasant memories – or were these dreams again.

He didn't want to sleep, he liked this feeling, but it felt so peaceful and comfortable that he drifted slowly towards a dream. The gentle touch was still there, but it was harder to work out where it was now. There was a definite insistence to this caress, not just a simple, delicate touch but an unmistakable exploring and a much stronger feeling of purpose to the contact.

When he woke, the feeling of contact was still there. Only he didn't just feel it on his leg. Instead, there was now a feeling of determination and a real sense of purpose – he was wanted.

The joining was a slow and restful time. He felt the warmth and the light coming and going in a regular and unrelenting way. The time of light was getting longer, and the feeling of warmth was extending throughout his body. But he couldn't feel his body. He knew he had one, he had always had it, and he had grown used to the way it felt. It wasn't as good as it had been, a few aches here and there, and he had been developing a growing sense of tiredness – he felt as if he should sleep again.

Later, when he woke, he knew something was different, he wasn't sure what it was, but he felt as though he had a purpose. The sense of touch was still there, but it was inside him, part of him, and he was part of it. All of him felt alive and well and growing.

< 3 >

He was more awake now and so much more aware – or was this still a dream? The warm breeze felt good; there was a gentle susurration in the grass all around him. He felt a rising strength in himself, but he also felt delicate, and it seemed as if part of him was standing and a part of him wasn't.

That was odd – but in dreams, anything can happen.

The feeling of strength seemed to grow along with his awareness, he could feel the strength in his body growing. His feet felt cool and solid, but his arms and his fingers felt as though they were catching the light. The light was good, it was more than warmth. It felt nourishing – could you eat light? He knew he should be hungry; they hadn't brought him any food for a long time now. But the light was good, and he didn't feel hungry.

The time of the light, he knew it was daylight now, grew longer and the periods of dark were shorter. He didn't feel the urge to sleep so much now; he felt an urgency to grow and a need for the light, but not sleep. He still couldn't see, but he felt as though he knew where everything was. He felt connected and part of the whole.

The whole what? The feeling of being part of the whole was almost overwhelming now – it was good, he knew it was good, and what he had always wanted, but what was it? The warmth and the sunlight were helping to make him feel well and rested; his feet felt a little damp, but the rest of him felt as though it could reach up and capture all the warmth and the light around him.

These were lazy days; he knew they were days, but they all seemed to run together. Sometimes it was warm and dry and dusty, but occasionally the rain washed over him, which felt good – cool and refreshing. After the rain, there was a clean freshness, and everything felt so alive. All around, he could feel the surge as everything around him seemed to feel the need to grow as much as it could. The sunlight, warmth, and rain made him feel ready for anything.

< 4 >

But then there was a day with a disturbance. He didn't know what was happening, but there seemed to be people, people near him. He could sense the people but not see them; he knew these were people, but he wasn't sure what they were doing. The small creatures that had set up home with him had gone noticeably quiet. There was the odd chirp from a young bird, but the older ones quickly shushed that, and the furry animals had all stopped feeding and moving.

Apart from the disturbance, the day turned into another gentle summer day. The disturbance ended, and the people went away again. The small creatures slowly emerged from wherever they had been hiding, the older ones were still scolding the young, but they were soon settling back into their normal routines. The sunshine warmed him and made him feel sleepy. Not the deep sleep of the cold and the dark, but a slow lazy nap in the summer sun.

When he woke, there was a difference. He felt it, he wasn't sure what it was, but something he felt had changed. The sun was getting lower, but it wasn't dark yet. He reached out and tentatively felt around him, he wasn't sure what it was he was looking for, but it was something new. He felt the same, perhaps a little different, but then most days, he did seem to change a little. The animals on the ground had found loose soil to explore, and the birds were busy checking for anything to eat.

Then as he stretched and felt his way, he came across something familiar, it was cloth. He hadn't felt cloth for some time now. His own clothes just didn't seem to be there anymore. He wasn't sure why, but he wasn't cold, and the clothes no longer felt important. This was new, though, not quite as soft as he remembered but it almost felt lived in. Almost unconsciously, he carried on gently teasing his way through the cloth then, and it was a shock, he realised it was another person. Had they put someone else in his room – that seemed odd they hadn't done that before. He withdrew when he found what he was feeling, but there was no reaction to his touch. Perhaps the other person was sleeping, he would meet them when they were awake, and he was.

< 5 >

There was another day of disturbance and another. On the days when there was a disturbance but always in distinct parts of the woods, he would try to reach out. If it was close, he could spread out and gently make contact, but often it took him some time to make contact and find out who had arrived. It felt good to meet all these new people; they didn't speak or say much and were often asleep, but he liked the quiet it let him listen to the trees and the birds and the animals.

They generally all got along once they had made contact. There were those who were a little quiet to start with, others were lost and confused, but most of them soon settled into this new way of being themselves. They didn't meet, at least not in the conventional sense, but they all seemed to be aware of each other and what the others were thinking. The newcomers all felt a little different; some felt prickly, some were strong, some were smooth or slender, but all had a feeling of life and growth.

People arrived in ones and twos throughout the year but always with a little disturbance and more people who left soon after. The disturbances soon seemed to fill the woods, or at least to take place all over it. Never too close, but also never so far away that between them they couldn't make contact. There was no organisation to this, just whoever was closest or could reach out and touch the new person.

Eventually, the disturbances seemed to stop, and no more new people arrived. However, the small creatures and birds were still there, they seemed happier now with fewer comings and goings, and that was good – it was peaceful again.

Later in the year, it began to get cooler, and the light didn't seem to last as long. It wasn't dark in the way it had been before, but he was beginning to feel the urge to move back down into the safety of the dark again. Perhaps it would soon be time to sleep again, but not just yet still one last thing to do.

< 6 >

It began soon after the rain. He knew it was rain, he had seen rain before, but this was different. He didn't so much see the rain as feel it washing over him and down to soak his feet. Why had they left him out in the rain they were normally so careful? But the rain felt good, refreshing and cleansing, softening the ground and giving him that last drink.

When it came, it was quite unexpected; he hadn't felt anything like this before, he seemed to be losing parts of himself – but it felt right; it was something he knew he had to do. The cool of the morning was replaced by a fleeting time of warmth and light, the misty time replaced by a clear, bright day before cooling once more for the night-time sleep.

Each day he lost a little more until one day, after a particularly cool night, he realised he had lost the leaves that soaked up the sunlight. He started to panic – if he could no longer hold the sunlight, how would he cope. He could feel the warmth on his body, but he didn't seem to be able to hold any of it. Maybe it really was time to sleep.

The sleep, when it arrived, took over every part of him. As he relaxed, he started to sink down to a dark, moist, and comfortable place. He could still feel the gentle chatter of the small creatures that seemed to keep him company these days, but even they were beginning to slow down and sleep more than they usually did.

Was it night-time again? This didn't feel like night-time. This felt far more important than that short sleep.

5. the illumination

this story is about finding a balance
between the dark and the illuminating.

As soon as the sun rose every morning, they were up to welcome it, singing songs of celebration for the light. And when the sun went down each evening they sang other songs, sad songs, songs of missing the light of the sun. They loved the light so very much.

They did not love the darkness. Once darkness fell every night, they would hurry to bed, since they could only bear the darkness when they were asleep. Even then, total darkness was frightening to them, and so they always kept a fire burning in every room.

The people's dearest wish was that the sun would not set in the evening, that darkness would never fall. But every day the sun set and they sang their sad songs and they endured the fearful, sad, strange darkness until they could greet the sun again the next day.

Now in this land were born two remarkable children. They were twins. One was a girl, and she seemed to shine from within. Whenever she entered a room, everything seemed to get a little brighter. And the people loved her very much.

The other was a boy, and he seemed to bring darkness with him. Whenever he entered a room, everything seemed a little dimmer. And the people did not like him. They feared him because he reminded them of the great darkness of the night. But although the people loved the girl and did not love the boy, the twins loved each other very much. And because the girl loved her brother so very much, the people mostly let him be even though they were afraid of him.

Now, as they grew, it became clear that these children were, in fact, magical children. The girl had the power to bring life back when it was harmed or lost. When she was a very small child, she could heal small cuts and bruises. When she grew a little older, she could heal broken bones and other larger hurts. And by the time she was a teenager, she could make the crops grow faster and larger and fuller. She could bring plants and animals that had died back to life. The people suspected she could even bring people back to life, but they were a little afraid to ask, and she did not offer.

The boy, on the other hand, had the power to calm and quiet anything. When he was a very small child, he could help his family go to sleep more quickly, thus saving them from the fear of the darkness. When he was a little older, he could calm animals when they were frightened and make them still. Sometimes, he would go first to an animal or a person who was hurt and help them to be calm enough for his sister's healing magic to work. And by the time he was a teenager, he could calm storms and winds and rains. He could bring anything to stillness.

The people's love for the light and fear of the darkness only grew with time, perhaps more strongly with the twins always before them to remind them.

And so one day, they decided to ask the girl for a favor. They asked her to see if her magic could hold the sun in the sky and stop the night from coming. The girl was reluctant, but after many, many months of being asked, she finally decided to try, just to get the people to leave her alone. One day, just as the sun was at its highest point, she went out onto the top of the highest hill in the land, and she threw her arms up into the sky, and she asked the sun to stop, to stay right there at the top of the sky forever.

She wasn't immediately sure that anything had happened. The sun usually moves so slowly. But before very long it became clear that something had happened. The sun had stopped in the sky.

The people were overjoyed. There was a big celebration. They sang all of their songs celebrating the sun. They loved the girl even more—at least at first. For the first week or so, everyone was happy and content.

But soon they began to get tired. Although they had always slept with a fire to ward off the darkness, sleeping in the full light of the sun was another thing altogether. They tossed and turned and woke up constantly. Some of them remembered that the boy could help with sleep, and asked for his aid, but his power of bringing sleep seemed to have disappeared along with the darkness.

After about a month, the exhausted, frustrated people began to see that this constant sunlight was a problem. Though they still loved the light, they began to wish that the sun would once again move in the sky. Each person at first thought that they were the only one who thought this. And given the people's love of the light and fear of the darkness, everyone was afraid, at first, to say anything about this growing longing for nighttime. But slowly, softly, as they began to confide in each other, they discovered that everyone felt this way. And they finally decided that something must be done.

They went back to the girl and asked her to get the sun to move again. It was her magic that had stopped it, and they figured her magic could make it move again. So, she went back up onto the top of the highest hill, threw her arms up into the sky and asked the sun to move. Nothing happened. She tried again. And a third time, but the sun stayed still. Sadly, she turned to the people and told them there was nothing she could do. There was a long moment of growing panic before the boy stepped forward. "Let me try," he said softly. Everyone thought about it for a moment and then decided this was a good idea.

So, he took his sister's place on the top of the highest hill, threw his arms up to the sky, and asked the sun to move. The sun began moving at once, rushing toward the western horizon. Within ten minutes, it had set, and within fifteen, it was full, dark night.

The people were caught off guard. They had all come out to the hill to see if the girl's magic would work. They had no fires lit—they hadn't needed them in weeks. They had nothing with them to light their way. They had never been outside at night before, and they were terrified.

At first, they tried rushing home to get away from the darkness, but they soon discovered that rushing when you can't see where you are going is a bad idea. They slowed down, but still peered at the ground, trying to get home as soon as they could. But then, one of them looked up. "Oh!" she exclaimed. "Look!" Everyone looked up, and then they all saw the stars for the first time. They had never been outside at night before, and had no idea of the incredible beauty of a sky full of stars. They all stopped hurrying toward their homes and stood and stared in wonder. And then they realized how very tired they were, and so slowly now, and with more reverence, they started home again. They all slept for a very long time.

The people rested and were glad, and appreciated the darkness for the first time in their lives. Eventually, the sun rose again. As it did, the people got out of their beds and sang their songs to celebrate the coming of the light. But at the end of the day, as the sun began to sink toward the horizon, they did not feel like singing their sad songs. Instead, one of the musicians began singing a new song, a slow, quiet song of thanksgiving for the night. And soon the others joined in. It became their new sunset song.

And the boy and the girl grew up to be a man and a woman, and both of them were now much beloved by the people. Looking at them, still the best of friends as well as siblings, the people remembered that light and darkness are best in balance.

6. magic and enchantment

free will magic and enchantment doodles/
free to color or darken (2/2)

MYSELF
YAS GIRL!
SUPPORT
YOUR LOCAL
GIRL GANG

JMN '17
XXX
#BLM

A Note

Thank You for giving it a read! This book has been a great journey, from writing fables and magical enchanting poetries to short stories and other prompts picked out of my own daily life, it is nothing but a short simple sweet read about the depths and simplicities that life holds.

For further queries you may write to me: advmeghakaushik[at]gmail.com

9 798888 151129

Printed by Libri Plureos GmbH in Hamburg,
Germany